KNIGHT'S MOVE

The Hunt for Marshal Tito 1944

DAVID GREENTREE

First published in Great Britain in 2012 by Osprey Publishing,
Midland House, West Way, Botley, Oxford, OX2 0PH, UK
44-02 23rd Street, Suite 219, Long Island City, NY 11101, USA

OSPREY PUBLISHING IS PART OF THE OSPREY GROUP

E-mail: info@ospreypublishing.com

© 2012 Osprey Publishing Ltd.

A CIP catalogue record for this book is available from the British Library

Print ISBN: 978 1 84908 601 1
PDF ebook ISBN: 978 1 84908 602 8
ePub ebook ISBN: 978 1 78096 461 4

Page layout by bounford.com
Index by Sharon Redmayne
Typeset in Sabon
3D BEVs by The Black Spot
Maps by bounford.com
Originated by PDQ Media Digital Solutions, Suffolk
Printed in China through Worldprint Ltd

12 13 14 15 16 10 9 8 7 6 5 4 3 2 1

Osprey Publishing is supporting the Woodland Trust, the UK's leading
woodland conservation charity, by funding the dedication of trees.

www.ospreypublishing.com

ACKNOWLEDGEMENTS

I would like to acknowledge the following for their help with the
production of this book: Ivo Vraničar and Katarina Jurjavčič from the
Slovenian Museum of Contemporary History, Martina Caspers from
the Bundesarchiv, Ted Nevill, Rolf Michaelis, Marc Rikmenspoel, Tommy
Natedal, Geir Brenden, Velimir Vuksic, Alex Kendrick, and David Campbell.
Thanks are also due to my uncle Colin Greentree, Anja Guergen, and Allison
Williams for help translating German, and to Marko Konen from the Vila
Bled for his perceptive insights into Yugoslavian history. Finally I would like
to express my gratitude to my father, Roy Greentree, for his patience and
understanding, and to my Canadian friend and comrade in Afghanistan,
Jason Toth, for his good humour. He truly does always laugh and joke
despite the circumstances.

ARTIST'S NOTE

Readers may care to note that the original painting from which the cover of
this book was prepared is available for private sale. All reproduction
copyright whatsoever is retained by the Publishers. All inquiries should be
addressed to:

mark@mrstacey.plus.com

The Publishers regret that they can enter into no correspondence upon this
matter.

CONTENTS

INTRODUCTION

In the early morning of 25 May 1944 Tito heard the screeching engines of two fighter aircraft tearing down the valley. He rushed out of his office – a small wooden shack built at the entrance of a cave that nestled into an escarpment overlooking the small town of Drvar in north-western Bosnia – to see Junkers 87 Stuka dive-bombers bank into a dive and plummet earthward to deliver their high-explosive ordnance onto houses in the town. Three days before, after a German Fieseler Storch aircraft had been seen flying over Drvar, the British military mission to his headquarters advised that a German aerial attack was imminent. Since 1941, to avoid the merciless fate German policy dictated for partisans, Tito had kept his men constantly on the move. In June 1943 he had a narrow escape after a German bomb killed many of his entourage; however, in November he felt secure enough to stop running, and established a new socialist government for Yugoslavia at Jajce in Bosnia. Paradoxically, the success of his movement made him more vulnerable than ever. German agents had discovered his new location and an offensive was launched to destroy his headquarters. As Tito continued to watch the aircraft twist and turn he noticed slower, straight-winged planes start to descend and out of others small, mushrooming flecks of white appear. The centrepiece of the attack, codenamed *Rösselsprung* (Knight's Move), was a daring glider and parachute assault, which could have only one purpose – to kill or capture him before he could make good an escape.

The German paratroopers that occupied those gliders and who were parachuting down into the heart of partisan power were members of the recently formed 500th SS Parachute Battalion. German Army Group F commander Generalfeldmarschall von Weichs, commander-in-chief for the Balkans, entrusted their commander Hauptsturmführer Rybka with this mission critical task. Many recruits to his unit were SS soldiers who had been punished for some misdemeanour and demoted, and success in this highly dangerous endeavour could lead to a restoration of rank and standing. However, they were being dropped into a cauldron, with the expectation that partisans would flood the area from all sides in an attempt to overwhelm them.

Rybka and his men would have to rely on ground units from Generaloberst Rendulic's 2nd Panzer Army to reach them before this happened.

Many of the paratroopers would have felt apprehensive during their approach to Drvar. Not only were they about to descend behind enemy lines, but they were also entering an unforgiving, inhospitable environment where both sides gave no quarter. In the 1920s and 30s the Serbian-dominated Yugoslavian government had done nothing to mollify ethnic rivalries that had long endured in the Balkans. In April 1941 military defeat by Germany heralded the arrival of an extreme Croatian regime in Zagreb, whose agenda was the expulsion, absorption or destruction of the Serbian people. Add to this a brutal German occupation policy that viewed resistance or assistance to those that did as punishable by death, as well as a racial intolerance that viewed Slavs as inferior, and an environment was created in which the fighting was often savage and unrelenting. If the operation did not unfold as planned, the SS paratroopers would be threatened with annihilation, but for von Weichs the prize was worth the risk and Himmler, keen to bask in the reflected glow of victories won by his men, authorized their use.

The operation was not embarked upon lightly. The plan could succeed only if the intelligence upon which it was founded was accurate and in Yugoslavia there was a rich vein of potential betrayers to provide human intelligence, potentially the most exploitable. Agent handlers from the Abwehr (German military intelligence) and from October 1943, men from the Brandenburg Regiment had been operating clandestinely among the local population. In March 1944 their sources told them Tito was in Drvar. The following month Hitler intervened and, impressed with Sturmbannführer Skorzeny's role in rescuing Mussolini from Gran Sasso mountaintop, sent the SS officer to hunt Tito down. Skorzeny was the leader of the SS Friedenthal Battalion – theoretically an elite unit established for operations behind enemy lines. The ability to properly utilize intelligence provided by the Brandenburgers and Skorzeny, as well as imagery and signals intercepts, would heavily influence the fate of the paratroopers, the partisans that rushed to Tito's aid, and Tito himself.

The German operation can be seen either as a last, desperate gamble, a final throw of the dice for the German High Command that routinely committed over 20 Axis divisions to combat the growing partisan movement and now launched a last-ditch attempt to stymie it, or a long-overdue example of traditional Blitzkrieg to remove at one stroke its talismanic leader.

Tito, far right, wearing marshal's uniform, poses for a British Army photographer in April 1944, part of a group of Allied journalists sent to his headquarters in Drvar. He is alongside some of his closest advisers, including his bespectacled intellectual mentor Kardelj. A cave overlooking the town was being used because of the threat from aerial bombardment. (Imperial War Museum, NA 15129)

Parachutists from the newly formed 500th SS Parachute Battalion collect their thoughts on the approach to Drvar whilst being transported in a Ju-52. This was their first operational jump and would be conducted into the heart of partisan territory. War correspondents including photographers were sent on the mission to exploit the presumed propaganda opportunity. (Slovenian Museum of Contemporary History)

Originally invaded by Hitler to protect the rear of the army as it stormed into Russia, many areas of Yugoslavia, in particular the territories of Bosnia-Herzegovina and Montenegro, had become ungovernable, despite the establishment of puppet regimes in Serbia and Croatia, the involvement of Italian and Bulgarian occupation troops to quell resistance, and the collaboration of Serbian Chetnik partisans. In early 1944, as the German army retreated from the Ukraine, guaranteeing communications in Yugoslavia was a top priority for von Weichs, but the resources available to him were dwindling. German formations were being sent to the Italian and Eastern Fronts, many Italian soldiers had joined the partisans after that country's capitulation in September 1943, and Italian weapons were being used to arm more partisan recruits. The encirclement of Tito's mobile formations had been attempted many times but Tito had always found a way of escaping. Weichs hoped a lightning strike at his headquarters would remove their inspirational leader, who he described as his 'most dangerous enemy', and deliver a mortal blow to the partisan movement.

Yugoslavia was also high on Churchill's list of priorities. Tito had long competed for arms from the allies with Mihailovic, the leader of the Serbian Chetniks and loyal follower of the Serbian King of Yugoslavia. In September 1943 Churchill dispatched one-star led military missions to the headquarters of both groups to assess their commitment to fight the occupiers. By November it was clear that the Chetniks were collaborating with the Nazis and that only Tito offered a real prospect of unhinging the German rear areas. Accusations made by the Soviets after the war that Britain purposely withheld intelligence derived from signals intercepts that pointed to the German airborne attack are groundless. America may have preferred to see Chetniks rather than communists in power after the war, but Churchill's policy to give Tito all the military supplies he wanted was adopted. He was also keen on landing an expeditionary force on the Dalmatian coast. Fitzroy MacLean, the British head of mission, made a reconnaissance of the area in December 1943. In May 1944 he was not in Drvar; however, others, including Major Randolph Churchill (the prime minister's son) and Major Vivian Street, were present, as were American and Soviet missions. When the Germans dropped from the sky the world's attention turned towards the town, as the outcome of the German attack could have consequences not only for the present strategic situation in the country, but also for its post-war political landscape.

ORIGINS

The German invasion of Yugoslavia was a strategic mistake, borne out of Hitler's fury after a palace coup in Belgrade overthrew the pro-Axis regent Prince Paul and replaced him with the young king-in-waiting Prince Peter, who favoured the Allies. On 6 April the terror bombing of Belgrade killed 10,000 civilians and heralded the start of Operation *Punishment*, an invasion designed to dismember the country. German armies crossed over the borders that the country shared with its many Balkan neighbours, who had all already joined the Axis, and quickly overwhelmed the regular Yugoslav army, which was still mobilizing and suffering from the wholesale desertion of some Croat regiments. On 17 April the Yugoslavs surrendered to von Weichs in Belgrade.

The German presence widened their zone of control around the Rumanian oilfields and secured access to mineral deposits, especially copper in Serbia and bauxite in Croatia. However, little thought had been given to military plans for the occupation and the Germans were keen to rely on their allies to provide garrison troops. The Italians, Bulgarians and Hungarians shared occupation duties in exchange for territory, and Croatia gained its independence under the fascist government of Pavelic, in the process acquiring half of Bosnia-Herzegovina at the expense of accepting Italian garrisons on the Dalmatian coast. Only in Serbia, where a puppet regime under General Nedic was established, did the Germans take more direct control, but the three front-line divisions there (60th Motorized, 4th Mountain and 294th Infantry) were soon dispatched to Russia, which Hitler invaded in June, and replaced by four infantry divisions formed from men born between 1907 and 1913 (the 704th, 714th, 717th and 718th).

Yugoslavia, the land of the united South Slavs, had been created in 1919 from the debris of the Austro-Hungarian Empire. The country comprised numerous subgroups, most prominently the Croats and Serbs, and was vulnerable to inter-ethnic rivalries. In the days of Empire Croats had been favoured over Serbs and now the Serbs wanted to dominate the new country. Into this mix emerged an industrial working class that was represented by a vociferous trade union movement, which the new Communist party attempted

6 APRIL 1941

Bombing of Belgrade heralds Axis invasion of Yugoslavia

to influence. Yugoslavian politics quickly polarized. In 1920 the Communist party was banned after their members killed the Minister of Interior. In 1928 a Serb shot dead the head of the Croat Peasant Party, prompting the King to dissolve parliament and suspend the constitution. A far-right Croat terrorist group called the Ustaše was founded under Pavelic, which operated out of Italy and in 1934 assassinated the King in Marseilles. The Communist party worked covertly to spread its influence but suffered from ideological bickering. In 1938 Tito, noted for having a common-sense approach, travelled incognito to Moscow to be the Yugoslav representative on the COMINTERN (Communist International) and upon his return to Yugoslavia in 1939 was made leader of the Communist party with Soviet approval.

In 1941, after the Yugoslavian collapse, Pavelic entered Zagreb and announced that the 'Serbs are alien elements on Croat territory. They are by their nature irreconcilable enemies of the Croat state.' Tito escaped Zagreb and travelled to Belgrade but operating in the city was too dangerous and in September he travelled south-west into the hills and called upon the 7,000 members of his Communist party to assist him. Tito's partisans competed with the royalist Chetniks[1] for Yugoslav soldiers that still wanted to fight. By the end of September 5,000 Chetniks and 15,000 partisans were under arms.

The tone of the partisan war soon became apparent. The Ustaše set about the destruction of Serbian enclaves in the expanded Croatia; resistance was met by bloody reprisals. On 16 September the German High Command (OKW) issued a directive stating that for every German life 'the general rule should be capital punishment of 50–100 communists' – a policy that was soon implemented. When on 18 October 1941 a partisan raid in Kragujevac killed ten German soldiers and wounded twenty, 5,000 male inhabitants of the town between the ages of 16 and 60 were shot. In August 1942 OKW Directive 46 went further, authorizing German soldiers to shoot anyone who supported the partisans or allowed them into their homes. Another OKW order, dated 16 December 1942, described partisans as a disease and stated that 'no German employed in Bandenbekampfung [war against bandits] can be made responsible for their actions before the courts'. On 22 December 1943 von Weichs directed that any active or passive resistance by civilians could result in them being 'shot as bandit helpers and their dwellings destroyed'. According to the historian Martin van Creveld the German army's emphasis on initiative at the lower level of command and strict adherence to orders meant that troops could 'be relied upon not only to fight hard but to commit any kind of atrocity'. Once the Axis occupier meted out this violence it could not be undone. Brigadeführer Kumm, an SS divisional commander in the Balkans, writing after the war, stated it was 'creating problems faster than we could alleviate them'. Tito was provided with more recruits and partisans were less reticent about meting out similar treatment of collaborators and Croatian soldiers.

Conversely the Chetniks adopted a deliberately non-provocative stance and their local commanders would, if it suited, collaborate with the Germans and Italians. The Germans benefited from the split in the resistance movements.

---

1 The name Chetnik came from the Serb cetas or companies that had fought the Turks since the Middle Ages.

Here Chetniks cooperate with senior SS officers in questioning the indigenous population. Chetniks sought a return to the monarchy but were willing to cooperate with the Germans to defeat the Communist partisans. In May 1943 Mihailovic reportedly approached the Germans through a senior Brandenburg officer intermediary, offering to provide a division to fight on the Eastern front if a Serbian state was restored; however, Hitler refused. (Alamy)

Tito and Mihailovic could not agree over joint action against the Germans. Their forces often skirmished with each other and the Chetniks even handed over captured partisans to the Germans. However, the Germans failed to fully capitalize on this situation. On 13 November, when Mihailovic had a meeting with a German Abwehr captain and mooted an alliance in exchange for arms, the German High Command rejected the offer.

German strategy showed an initial lack of appreciation about what the partisan threat could grow to be. In late 1941 the First Offensive by two divisions in Serbia succeeded in pushing Tito out of his headquarters in Uzice, where the partisans controlled a small arms and munitions factory. By sheer chance Tito was nearly captured leading the rearguard when explosives on a bridge over which German tanks were crossing failed to explode, but he successfully led a withdrawal by 2,000 partisans into the sanctuary of the mountains of eastern Bosnia, where he organized the first proletarian brigades.

The Germans' principal concerns – to keep communications links open and exploit mineral deposits – helps explain their failure to nip the partisan threat in the bud. Their moves against the partisans were reactionary and relied on spreading fear and terror to stop locals assisting the resistance. In January 1942 during the Second Offensive the Germans were happy to depend on Croat and Italian forces but their late arrival and poor performance allowed Tito to escape south to Foca near the Montenegrin border, albeit after losing 50 per cent of his force. In Montenegro the Italians were confined to the three major towns and at times openly allied themselves with the Chetniks. The Third Offensive, between April and June 1942 by two German and two Italian divisions, again lacked coordination, and the

18 OCTOBER 1941

5,000 men in Kragujevac shot in reprisal for partisan raid

partisans escaped through the encircling troops, embarking on a long march into Croat-controlled north-west Bosnia, where hard-fought victories were won over local Croat forces.

In Bosnia Tito was able to recruit from those who suffered from the Ustaše reign of terror. Many Croats detested the ethnic cleansing policies of the Zagreb regime and joined the partisans. Whilst the Chetniks were exclusively Serb, Tito's appeal was pan-ethnic. By November 1942 two mobile partisan divisions, each of approximately 4,000 men, were ready and another eight were forming. Tito's challenge was to have sufficient weapons and ammunition to arm them. That month he established a political wing, the Anti-Fascist Council of the National Liberation of Yugoslavia (AVNOJ), which gathered for its first meeting at Bihac.

The Germans were learning their lesson of relying on their allies and recruited three Croatian infantry divisions under German leadership. They also formed the 7th SS Prinz Eugen Mountain Division from the 700,000 ethnic Germans that lived in Yugoslavia and whom the Army Group E chief-of-staff described as 'superior to all other Germans in their knowledge of the nature and fighting methods of their enemy'. The division was used on search-and-destroy missions. Partisan Milo Stavic stated these 'traitors in the SS were ruthless; killing prisoners always'.

Overall, however, the Germans found there were not enough well-trained troops to follow up search-and-clear operations with hold operations, and the use of Special Forces to more effectively target the partisans was considered. In 1940 in the Low Countries German paratroopers had proven effective in dealing with Dutch and Belgian fixed positions but after the drop on Crete in 1941 Hitler banned their large-scale use because of the losses

The partisans had to keep mobile to survive and sought to surprise Axis troops by appearing where least expected. Partisan formations, winding their way through woods and across rivers and mountains in long lines, were difficult to detect. (Cody Images)

Information collected from human intelligence sources was integral to the effective prosecution of the anti-partisan campaign in Yugoslavia. Many civilians cooperated with the German occupiers against Tito's Communist partisans and from 1943 specialist teams sought to cultivate them as covert agents to move freely in partisan-controlled territory and collect intelligence on enemy dispositions and intentions. (Bundesarchiv, Bild 101I-005-0012-18)

incurred through landing lightly armed men on occupied positions with no immediate relief. The infiltration of smaller groups of elite soldiers, by parachute or glider if necessary, trained in disguise, deception and sabotage, offered a much smaller risk.

Section IIc of the Abwehr was responsible for conducting sabotage and other special missions behind enemy lines and in 1939 had established a unit for this purpose, known as the Brandenburgers after the location of their barracks, and consisting of ethnic Germans who spoke local languages. In late 1940, after developing a reputation for daring missions in the Low Countries, the unit expanded into a regiment, and from 1941–42 continued to win new laurels in Russia. In December 1942 the Brandenburgers had been expanded into a division and on 1 April 1943 this was placed under the direct control of the German Armed Forces High Command operations staff. That spring two battalions deployed to Yugoslavia (five were in Greece and another four were fighting partisans in Russia). In November an additional four battalions (including the 2nd Regiment, which fought with 1st Mountain Division in Bosnia) followed and their number still included specialists whose role was to infiltrate behind enemy lines.

Special Forces operations, more than any other, were intelligence-driven. Interception of partisan and Allied communications assisted the identification of partisan concentrations and locations where Allied airdrops were expected. Exploiting human sources was also central to intelligence collection; however, German appreciation of such information had a long chequered history, coloured by a traditional aristocratic attitude that viewed people willing to betray their country as dishonourable. The Abwehr's Human Intelligence teams, known as Frontaufklärungskommando (FAK), were responsible for running agents but from mid-1943 the Brandenburgers were beginning to excel in this arena and information from their sources became central to the efficient targeting of partisan forces.

INITIAL STRATEGY

By 1943 the Germans realized that the partisans were now a major threat rather than a minor irritant and were deploying more security forces to the Balkans. Operations orders still stressed the 'securing of bauxite and copper mining regions' and the control of towns and major communications links, but now German offensives attempted to exterminate the partisans en masse by bringing in mountain troops whose training and specialist equipment – boots, clothing and weapons – made them capable of operating effectively in rough terrain and cold weather. German security forces also benefited from an integrated communications network, which relied on radio transmitters and was not vulnerable to partisans cutting telephone cables. The SS operated wireless transmission network stations in Belgrade, Graz and Ljubjlana, and mobile radio vans that used short-wave radios were used in the field. These communications facilitated the rapid deployment and coordination of units during operations. The Germans also realized that the effective use of air superiority was a prerequisite for success on the ground, especially in the mountainous terrain of Yugoslavia. Aircraft facilitated the relaying of

The Henschel 126, capable of short take-off and slow speeds, was designed as a reconnaissance aircraft but could also deliver up to 330lb of bombs. Behind the pilot sat an observer who operated a machine gun. First seeing service in 1938 during the Spanish Civil War, in 1942 it had been replaced in the front line by the Fieseler Storch; however, the aircraft was still being used in the Balkans. (Bundesarchiv, Bild 101I-565-1425-11A, Fotograf: Schnitzer)

information, observation of troop movements and marking of targets, as well as dropping of ordnance, often on targets identified by human intelligence sources. In one instance in November 1943 a captured German plane was being used to transport a high-profile partisan delegation to North Africa. Just prior to take-off, a German aircraft swooped down and destroyed the plane. In another incident in April 1944 a bomb dropped from a small monoplane destroyed the building that Gosnjak, the Croatian partisan leader, was using as his headquarters. Luckily he had found out his location had been betrayed and evacuated prior to the attack.

The German assumption that it was better to kill rather than convert an insurgent persisted. In 1943 Obergruppenführer Phleps, the commanding officer of V SS Mountain Corps, said that in contested areas 'the entire population ... must be considered rebel sympathizers'. After the war the War Crimes tribunal reported that villages suspected of collaboration would be 'reduced to rubble and ashes' and the inhabitants evacuated on foot to the rear. 'Some of the aged would die en route; of the others some would be executed as bandit suspects or bandit helpers after screening by the [security service]; the remainder would be sent to the Reich for labour.' In such an environment resistance grew and attitudes hardened.

Operation *Weiss*

By 1943 a second front in Europe was expected and Hitler wanted no ready-made bridgeheads for the enemy. He summoned the Croatian leader Pavelic to his Russian headquarters at Vinnitsa and ranted how Croatian troops should be fighting Russians rather than partisans. The German Fourth Offensive – codenamed Operation *Weiss* – represented a more determined effort than what went before. Luftwaffe General Löhr, the current Commander-in-Chief Southeast Europe, was tasked with encircling and annihilating Tito's mobile divisions. In December 1942 Directive 47 bound all Axis troops under his unified command. On 3 January 1943 he attended a conference in Rome with Italian, Croatian and Chetnik commanders, and soon after 140,000 men began to close in on 30,000 partisans. Five Italian divisions and 12,000 Chetniks advanced from the south and west, whilst the Germans – 7th SS, 369th (Croatian), 187th, 714th, and 717th divisions – supported by three Croat brigades came in from the north and east.

Tito knew from his spies in the Chetnik camp that the Germans planned an encirclement and marched his forces south, sending them on a 100-mile trek to the mouth of the Neretva Valley on the northern border of Montenegro. He realized 'we must not let the enemy force us by clever tactics onto the defensive. We must make up for the loss of one area by the conquest of a larger and more

NOVEMBER 1942

Tito's partisan force reaches two-division strength

Until late 1943 Germany relied on its allies to provide most of the occupation forces. For Operation *Weiss* Hitler instructed Löhr 'to maintain close liaison with Italian commanders concerned in planning and carrying out operations', however the four Italian divisions involved failed to close the ring. At Prozor 1,000 Italians were captured and many massacred, leading Hitler to warn Mussolini of the 'innate cunning and deceitfulness of the Slavs'. (Bundesarchiv, Bild 101I-201-1563-17A, Fotograf: Wurm)

important area.' Three thousand sick and wounded, and many thousands of refugees accompanied the column. Typhus was raging, food was short, the weather was cold and thick snow covered the ground but these conditions did not stop the 1st and 3rd Partisan Divisions destroying the Italian Murge division at Prozor on 15 February, capturing arms, supplies, guns and even tanks, which prompted Hitler to write to Mussolini how it was 'both impressive and alarming to observe what progress the insurgents have made with their organization'.

The Germans continued their pursuit. On 28 February, to deceive the Germans that he would not continue south, Tito destroyed the bridges over the Neretva and attacked north with a portion of his force. Crossing the river offered the only way out, however, and on 6 March at Jablanica the 2nd Proletarian Division attacked southwards, whilst the 1st formed the rearguard and the 3rd secured the flank. The river, 70 yards wide and with high, steep banks, had been made into a torrent by the melting snows. A blockhouse sited at the wreckage of an old railway bridge was taken, and during the night a rough plank bridge, lashed together from telegraph poles, was improvised through its remains, which allowed men and mules to cross. By 15 March 20,000 partisans and 4,000 wounded were over the river. The clash with the Chetniks, occupying the slopes of Mount Prenj in Montenegro, was unavoidable and completely one-sided. The partisans hunted them down and many Chetniks changed sides. The consequences of relying on Allied troops were laid bare. In retribution the Germans destroyed 14 villages around Jablanica and deported 2,000 captives to Germany.

Operation *Schwarz*

Tito had escaped from Bosnia but he now lay cornered in the barren terrain of Montenegro. Lack of weapons, Tito conceded, forced his men 'to attack a town or village not because of strategic importance, but simply in order to capture arms and ammunition'. The Germans brought in more specialist troops, including the 1st Mountain Division and the Brandenburgers, and in May launched the Fifth Offensive – codenamed Operation *Schwarz* – with 50,000 German (including 704th, 718th, 719th Infantry Divisions, grandiosely redesignated the 104th, 118th and 119th Jäger Divisions and given mountain troop uniforms, and the 7th SS Mountain Division), 40,000 Italian, and 30,000 Croat and Bulgarian troops to eliminate Tito's 20,000 partisans concentrated around Mount Durmitor.

The Germans would succeed if they could deny the partisans freedom of movement, force them to fight and take advantage of their limited weaponry and ammunition supplies. The Axis advanced from all sides, this time deploying lighter battle groups and mobile shock units ahead of the main body and at times supplying them by air. General Rubler, commanding officer of the 118th Jäger Division, told his men 'every partisan is to be shot. If the local inhabitants are hostile to German forces, treat them with the greatest possible brutality and severity. If they are friendly, harness them in the struggle against the partisan. Destroy anything that could be of slightest use to the partisans.'

Tito was bottled up on the Piva plateau. If he retreated further into Montenegro he would probably never return to Bosnia. He took the bull by the horns and advanced north across the Maglic massif into the maelstrom. The Sutjeska river flowed around the western and northern faces of the Maglic and by 5 June the Germans, including the 7th SS and 118th Divisions, occupied the far bank, except for the most inaccessible section, a 3-mile canyon that in places had perpendicular cliffs dropping 3,000 feet and was crowned by thick forest. Partisans were defending one end of this stretch of river from the town of Suha and close by here on the night of 7 June Tito led his men across, using frail rope bridges and under heavy shelling, before climbing up a narrow path cut into the cliff face on the far bank.

The next day the weather cleared and Stuka and Dornier bombers methodically dropped ordnance across the hillsides. One landed near Tito and a British mission that had recently arrived by parachute to confirm reports of partisan resistance. Tito was wounded in the left arm by shrapnel and his dog, Lux, was killed by the full impact of the blast. From the mission Captain Stewart was killed and Captain Deakin wounded in the right leg. However, German airpower could not stop the partisan attack. The 1st Proletarian Division proceeded to route a battalion of the 369th (Croatian) Division and punch through the German line, creating space for other partisan units to follow. The 3rd Proletarian Division, which was bringing up the rear, could not fully take advantage of this window of opportunity; their commander was killed and their wounded, who had to be left behind, were slaughtered. Despite this setback, by the end of the month Tito was back in Bosnia and the partisans fanned out to spread revolt.

The Germans, realizing Tito was cornered, had come close to destroying his mobile formations. Eight thousand men of their number had been killed. However, Tito kept his forces on the move and succeeded in re-entering Bosnia by the narrowest of margins. He then dispersed his formations so no single offensive could again threaten to eliminate his main fighting force.

Sixth Offensive

In September 1943 the surrender of Italy presented the partisans with a huge opportunity and they took full advantage. Italy had 14 divisions in Yugoslavia plus elements of four more; most were on the Dalmatian coast where the arms dumps were located. The partisans disarmed ten, distributed the weapons to 80,000 new partisan recruits and formed Italian volunteers into two divisions.

Large areas of Bosnia and Montenegro were especially hard to transit through and mountain troops were best suited to the terrain. In Montenegro, described by MacLean as a 'tangle of mountains, forests and rock strewn uplands', even Tito admitted 'difficulties of terrain and natural obstacles proved a disadvantage to us, and an advantage to the enemy'. (Bundesarchiv, Bild 1011-204-1721-04, Fotograf: Przibilla)

By year's end 290,000 partisans were organized into eight mobile corps and 26 other divisions, spread out all over Yugoslavia. On 29 November at its second plenary meeting at Jajce the AVNOJ proclaimed its legitimacy as Yugoslavia's proper constitutional body and recognized neither the King nor the government in exile. Tito was elected Prime Minister and made Minister of Defence with the rank Marshal of Yugoslavia. By the end of 1943 he established what he symbolically called a liberated area, bordered by Knin-Jajce-Bihac-Banja Luka. With the intention of staying put and in preparation for air raids he built underground rooms in the woods. Now the Dalmatian coast was under partisan control, he expected an Allied invasion.

By late 1943 eight partisan divisions and two corps had been formed as the shock formations of the Yugoslav Army of National Liberation. There were also numerous other local battalions. Discipline was inculcated through political instruction rather than drill. Communist ideology emphasized the equality of women and by 1945 approximately 10 per cent of partisans were female. (Cody Images)

The Germans regrouped and established a new command in Belgrade, Army Group F, headed by Generalfeldmarschall von Weichs, who controlled all German forces in Yugoslavia and Albania, and was also Supreme Commander Southeast in charge of Löhr's Army Group E in Greece. In Yugoslavia he had 200,000 German troops plus 160,000 Bulgarians and Croats, organized into ten German divisions, five divisions officered by Germans but with non-German soldiers (the 369th, 373rd, and 392nd – Croat formations, a Cossack division and a Bosnian Muslim SS division), four Bulgarian divisions, various Croatian units, and 50 static battalions. Weichs' principal formation was 2nd Panzer Army headed by Generaloberst Rendulic, which consisted of XV Mountain Corps, XXI Mountain Corps, V SS Mountain Corps and LXIX Corps.

In November 1943 von Weichs launched the Sixth Offensive to retake Dalmatia. If the partisans retained control of the coast, Allied supplies by sea would flow freely and Churchill might be persuaded to land ground forces. By January 1944 all the islands had been recaptured except for Vis, the furthest offshore, where a British commando brigade and a partisan brigade established a base and built an airstrip. In February the Germans also advanced against Jajce and forced Tito to relocate his headquarters further south to Petrovac, prior to a further move to the logging town of Drvar in the Unac valley.

Target Tito

The Germans no longer underestimated the dangers the partisans in general and Tito in particular represented. Earlier attempts at surrounding Tito's mobile formations had failed. The deteriorating situation now led them to focus on the partisan leadership, and command and control structure. Intelligence collection assets consisted of three different agencies running human intelligence sources, signals intercept units and reconnaissance aircraft. The Abwehr's FAK 201, composed of ten Frontaufklärungstruppe (FAT), was under the direct control

6 SEPTEMBER 1943

500th SS Parachute Battalion created for anti-partisan ops

of Army Group F's intelligence staff/Abwehr officer (Ic/AO). The FAT were small teams of approximately ten agent handlers (in German termed *schleusender* – literally 'sluicers') that developed contacts with local communities and inserted agents into enemy territory. Upon their return agents would be debriefed by members of the FAT, who would telephone immediate results to the Ic/AO and follow this up with a written report. No figures for the Balkans are available but in late 1944 feedback from analysts about reports from the Russian Front, which were derived from approximately 800 deployed agents, was mixed; only one quarter were regarded as 'usable' or 'very valuable'. The 2nd Panzer Army specifically operated FAT 176.

In Yugoslavia the Brandenburgers rather than the FAT were being more successful collecting information about Tito's whereabouts. In October 1943 a team from the 1st Battalion of the 4th Brandenburg Regiment under Oberleutnant Kirchner started to operate with local Chetniks under their commanders Drenovic and Tesavonic, operating 10–20 forward reconnaissance groups in partisan-controlled areas, and developing contacts with anti-communist farmers that could move comparatively freely.

Kirchner's men, including Germans with Middle Eastern experience, had originally been tasked with dropping into Kurdistan but when this mission was cancelled they were deployed to Banja Luka with attached Serbo-Croat linguists.

In November 1943 Kirchner had discovered Tito was in Jajce attending the AVNOJ annual general meeting and recommended infiltrating Brandenburgers accompanied by Chetniks dressed up in partisan uniform. Rendulic, who did not command Kirchner and perhaps resented him, was not convinced. According to the historian Slavko Odic, another plan to blow up Tito with a letter bomb was suggested. The intention was to murder a couple of prisoners, dress them up in British uniforms and throw them out of an aircraft with defective parachutes; on one would be a letter personally addressed to Tito. The

Generaloberst Dr Lothar Rendulic was born in Austria of Croatian parentage. He came from a military family and served in the Austro-Hungarian army during the Great War. He had joined the Austrian Nazi party before the 1938 Anschluss with Germany. An infantryman, in August 1943 he became commander of the nominally named 2nd Panzer Army. (Bundesarchiv, Bild 146-1995-027-32A, Fotograf: Krucker)

Soldiers from the Brandenburg Division, as well as running agents and debriefing locals, could also conduct reconnaissance missions from bases hidden deep inside the woods. (Bundesarchiv Bild 101I-005-0032-11)

plan was dropped. In December a Yugoslavian specialist Hauptmann Böckl took charge of Kirchner's men but in February 1944 was transferred for some misdemeanour. Major Benesch then took over and reorganized the teams into five units that became part of his 'Wildschutz' unit. Personnel wore typical farmers' garb, dressed up as Croat officers or even pretended to be partisans wearing Italian uniforms, and his group successfully tracked Tito to Drvar.

The Benesch group also pinpointed partisan locations for immediate targeting by motorized infantry from the Brandenburg Division. This was possible because signalmen accompanied them and transmitted daily intelligence reports. In May 1944 when Skorzeny was threatening to poach Brandenburgers their commanding officer defended their *raison d'être*: 'The Brandenburg division was created as a special unit for offensive operations. Since the German Armed Forces have been fighting on the defensive, it has adapted to this changing situation and has become the "OKW's standing anti-partisan unit."' He stated the division 'can only carry out its assigned tasks when it has the support of a sufficient cadre of fighting interpreters and recruited natives'. He suggested organising such men – of the 15,000 men in the unit approximately 1,000 were bilingual – into 'patrol corps' to carry out operations alongside each regiment of the division.

German intelligence efforts were also assisted by the interception of partisan radio communications. In the summer of 1943 a signals intercept detachment under Hauptmann Wollny moved from Salonika to Belgrade and within a couple of months was deciphering radio messages; however, determining the precise location of partisans was difficult because they were always on the move. When Tito installed his headquarters in Drvar that changed, and in March 1944 a constant stream of radio traffic suggested his headquarters was located in the town. The use of radios by the British mission also helped. According to Hilary King, MacLean's signals officer, the Germans were able to locate them through radio direction finders because the British mission were communicating directly with other British liaison teams in Yugoslavia rather than routing signals through SOE in Cairo or Bari. From 24 March XV Mountain Corps intelligence maps showed Tito's headquarters at Drvar; however, the precise whereabouts of Tito's personal quarters was unknown.

The SS now sought to steal the limelight. From 1943 the counterintelligence department of the SS Security Service, created in 1939 to collect intelligence for the Nazi party, sought to place agents in the Balkans and also controlled the SS Sonderkommando (Special Training Unit) Oranienburg, established in January 1940 to be the equivalent of the Brandenburgers. However, the unit was only 70 men strong and not until 1943 was it expanded into a battalion and renamed the SS Sonderkommando Friedenthal, after the town north of Berlin where it was barracked. According to the historian Philip Blood the unit was recruited from 'long term prisoners, dishonourably discharged from the SS and serving sentences of hard labour in concentration camps'. In April 1943 Sturmbannführer Skorzeny transferred into the SS Security Service to take command. A year later when he arrived in the Balkans the challenge was to ensure his activities were aligned within the existing intelligence collection apparatus.

In theory this should not have been difficult because the SS had been placed in charge of intelligence collection. On 12 February 1944 Hitler decreed that the Abwehr would be disbanded and subsumed into the SS Security Service. The SS had looked on the Abwehr with envious eyes and, helped by associations some senior Abwehr figures had with anti-Nazi conspirators, was able to cast the organization as disloyal. However in May 1944 FAK 201 was still subordinated to the army and the Brandenburg Division was still under OKW auspices. Whilst the SS had officially been given control of military intelligence, in practice the rivalries between the SS and other organizations were still very much being played out.

Skorzeny's orders to seize Tito dead or alive came directly from Hitler. In April he flew to Belgrade and with two NCOs from his battalion drove in his Mercedes to Zagreb. For four weeks he conducted patrolling in Bosnia and heard that a partisan deserter named Tetaric from I Proletarian Corps had betrayed the location of Tito's personal quarters, which he said were in a cave overlooking Drvar. He also found out 6,000 partisans were in the vicinity and an escort battalion of 350 men were guarding him and concluded that infiltrating a small force disguised as partisans into Tito's headquarters offered the only hope of success. Like the Brandenburgers he volunteered to lead men from his unit on such a mission and sent his second in command Hauptsturmführer von Foelkersam to suggest this to Generaloberst Rendulic. Rendulic told von Foelkersam that von Weichs' wanted to launch an offensive supported by an airborne drop on Tito's headquarters and dismissed him. The use of parachutists, which had recently been used against British forces in the Dodecanese islands with great success, was under consideration.

After the Brandenburgers identified Tito at Drvar, Rendulic's intelligence officer (Ic) sought to gather as much information as possible about his precise

Sturmbannführer Skorzeny was a mechanical engineer in the Waffen-SS who had no background in intelligence collection. He was scornful of German generals who he thought 'saw in me only an undesirable competitor'. In his opinion the Drvar operation failed 'through the petty jealousy of an officer avid of laurels' (a reference to Rendulic). Behind and to the left of Skorzeny is Hauptsturmführer Foelkersam, an ex-Brandenburger who in 1942 had infiltrated the Maikop oilfields in the Caucasus, and in 1943 transferred to the SS. (Bundesarchiv Bild 101I-680-8283-30A, Fotograf: Faupel)

OCTOBER
1943

Brandenburgers
begin anti-
partisan ops
with local
Chetniks

location. However, it seems that the Ic failed to determine the existence of Tito's cave. The Ic's position within the German staff hierarchy was not an enviable one. The intelligence function was subordinated to operations, and a good operations officer was expected to be able to determine enemy dispositions and intentions. At Army and Army Group level it was regarded as a stepping stone for an officer from the General Staff, who may only have attended a six-week course on intelligence matters, prior to a future appointment as an operations staff (Ia) or chief of staff. (At Corps or Divisional level a more experienced reservist probably filled the appointment.) A harmonious working relationship between the commanding officer and the Ic was essential if intelligence collection was to be conducted effectively.

500th SS Parachute Battalion

On 6 September 1943 the 500th SS Parachute Battalion was formed in Chlum, near Prague, for the purpose of carrying out special anti-partisan operations. Two-thirds were SS men who had been court-martialled for minor violations of military discipline and had been serving prison sentences, many of them in the SS Polizei penal camp in Danzig-Matzkau. As early as 1941 the SS Main Office discussed arrangements to form these men, who would be termed Bewahrungschutzen ('probationary soldiers'), into 'verlorener Haufen' (a term from the Middle Ages describing a unit established from sentenced offenders that hoped to gain financial rewards and fame but expected considerable losses). In early 1943 the SS Main Office had examined the cases of 600 volunteers for 'front probation'. The camp commandant was to assess their suitability but Himmler directed that all would serve in the SS Parachute Battalion. Entry criteria stipulated recruits had to be 160–185cm (5ft 3in–6in) tall, younger than 30 for junior NCOs and privates, and not prone to airsickness or stuttering.

Many soldiers hoped to distinguish themselves in combat, have their previous rank restored and earn a chance to return to their old unit. One recruit was Sturmmann Paul Firley, who had served with the 6th SS Nord Division in Finland. When he failed to show up for guard duty in Russia he had been sent to Danzig-Matzkau. He would go on to distinguish himself in combat

An SS volunteer described the probationary soldiers as 'a large spectrum of characters … most fit in without a problem, and were happy to have escaped the penal camp'. Many had little hope for the future but 'when they noticed that the SS members not previously convicted were to go into mission along with them, their opinion changed'. (Tommy Natedal via Marc Rikmenspoel)

with the battalion but choose not to return to his old unit. Another recruit, a Norwegian called Gunnar Baardseth serving in the SS Norge Regiment on the Eastern Front, had been confined in the military wing of Dachau concentration camp after shooting himself in the foot, and he was one of four Norwegians recruited into the battalion.

The SS Main Office also encouraged men from other SS units to volunteer and directed commanding officers not to refuse them permission. Many officers and NCOs came from the SS Das Reich and Leibstandarte Divisions, who happened to be convalescing away from the front after minor injuries or illnesses. Some volunteers did not realize the battalion consisted of disciplinary cases. In October 1943 when NCOs from the SS Das Reich Division and Oberstürmführer Fischer from the SS Gebirgsjäger training and replacement unit arrived at Chlum they observed soldiers wearing black collar patches without SS runes who had no displays of rank or decorations. When told these men were 'verlorener Haufen' one of the NCOs, Unterscharführer Karl Pichler, told how they were 'flabbergasted' and 'wanted to be transferred back to our old units' but were kicked out of the commander's quarters and 'with this we were dismissed and became Fallschirmjäger.' The commander was 33-year-old Sturmbannführer Herbert Gilhofer, an SS officer with previous experience of anti-partisan operations in Russia.

Others who volunteered included Hans-Joachim Draeger, an NCO in the 5th SS Wiking Division who had served in Russia in 1942. In 1943 he was attending the SS cavalry school in Warsaw when he saw a memorandum 'requesting SS officers to volunteer for a newly forming unit, a parachute battalion'. Together with his comrade Oberstürmführer Leifheit he volunteered. Both would be responsible 'for interviewing the new men and deciding which ones were considered fit to serve in an elite unit'. He described how not all recruits sent to the unit were taken: 'The ones we considered unfit were declared to be unacceptable for parachute training by the Battalion Doctor, and so were sorted out.'

On 1 December 1943 the battalion mustered 1,140 men and was fully motorized, possessing 100 trucks and 38 motorcycles. Unlike its Luftwaffe equivalent there were five instead of four infantry companies (three rifle companies, a heavy-weapons company and a replacement company) as well as a large headquarters company. The heavy-weapons company had 81mm mortar, machine-gun, 75mm recoilless rifle and flamethrower platoons. That month infantry training was completed and the unit commenced parachute training in Serbia. The battalion had transferred to Mataruschka-Banja in Serbia for parachute jump training with Fallschirmspringerschule III, which had been transferred from Braunschweig to avoid Allied bombing. By 8 February the battalion was available for airborne operations. In March a plan to drop them on Vis was abandoned only because of a developing crisis in Hungary.

Three weeks of ground school was spent practising landing drills. Unterscharführer Pichler described how a familiarization flight in a Ju-52 transport plane and six obligatory jumps followed, the first from 600m 'then each time 100 metres less'. The students were told 'that each person could refuse a jump three times. After the third refusal he would be transferred back to his former unit.' Pichler told how in April 1944 100 recruits were returned to Chlum. (Tommy Natedal via Marc Rikmenspoel)

8 FEBRUARY 1944

500th SS Parachute Battalion fully operational

THE PLAN

Early in 1944 von Weichs lost two divisions to the Italian Front and four to Hungary, and needed to find out new ways of doing more with less. German strategy continued to revolve around the encirclement and annihilation of partisan concentrations. However, according to Brigadeführer Kumm search-and-clear operations were being replaced by more focused direct attacks and pursuit operations. He described how once a partisan unit was located through intelligence, a probing force would attempt to fix the enemy whilst flanking units 'would pivot around the enemy, chasing them into the line of fire of the stationary unit'. Artillery fire would be called down 'behind the partisans preventing their escape, forcing them to stand and fight' and then be walked back thereby 'constricting the ring until the surviving partisans broke for cover'. A lane was temporarily kept free of fire to encourage a breakout and 'then bombing, artillery or machine gun fire' would be called down on them and those that remained in the cauldron. With these new tactics the Germans tried to prevent the partisans from melting away into the mountains.

In March 1944 Tito pushed II and III Partisan Corps from Bosnia into southern Serbia. Bulgarian troops were overrun but von Weichs brought in reserves, including the 500th SS Parachute Battalion, and launched Operation *Maibaum* (Mayflower) to stop the partisans from retreating across the River Drina north-east of Sarajevo. On 6 April 26-year-old Hauptsturmführer Rybka, who had previously served in the 6th SS Nord Mountain Division, replaced Gilhofer, who was promoted and transferred to the 10th SS Frundsberg Division. The V SS Mountain Corps units, which included the SS Prinz Eugen Division, occupied river valleys and main roads, and pressed partisans up against the river Drina but many escaped across the mountains. On 10 May the operation ended and the paratroopers returned to barracks. Tito realized that he was not yet strong enough to operate in the rolling hills of the Serbian countryside.

On 6 May von Weichs ordered Rendulic to prepare 2nd Panzer Army for an offensive into the Knin-Jajce-Bihac-Banja Luka-liberated area. OKW told von Weichs to make Tito his focus and that unlike any previous attacks

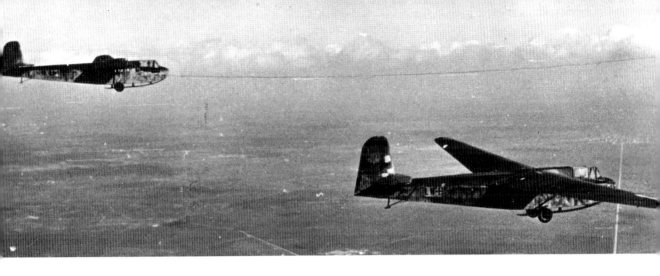

a parachute battalion would be provided to land at Drvar to capture him. On 10 May the SS officially released their parachute battalion for the operation. From his operational reserve Weichs committed the 92nd Motorized Regiment, the 202nd Panzer Company and the 4th Brandenburg Regiment.

The operational commander would be Generalleutnant Leyser, the commander of the XV Mountain Corps. From his headquarters at Knin he would control SS, Army, Luftwaffe and Croat troops. The corps operations order of 21 May explained the main components of the plan. On 25 May the enemy was to be attacked 'in an encircling operation using paratroops and our Air Force with the aim of destroying the enemy leadership, supply bases and headquarters in the area of Drvar-Petrovac and all enemy groups found in the area'. Because Tito was the target, the order considered 'the success of the operation will be of the greatest significance for the conduct of the war in the interior of the country as well as in the coastal areas'.

In total, five motorized columns would converge on Drvar. From the east, 43 miles (70km) from Drvar, the 7th SS Prinz Eugen Division 'with a regimental group and an assault battalion of *panzergrenadiers* under command, will smash through the enemy resistance east of the Sana river and will then advance on a broad front between the Sana and the Unac'. There they were 'to take out supply bases as well as prevent the flight eastwards of the beaten enemy groups and headquarters'. Specifically from the north-east 'the assault battalion with Panzer Company No. 202 under command will drive from Banja Luka towards Kljuc' and from the south-east 'the regimental group of 7th SS will drive from Jajce along the railways and roads'.

From the west a regimental group (Battle Group William) from the 373rd (Croatian) Infantry Division located on the Una river was to 'advance at best speed via Trubar to Drvar and there relieve, at whatever cost and on the same day, SS Paratroop Battalion 500 in Drvar'. For this important mission 'battle group William is to be made as strong as possible (artillery, heavy weapons, Engineers)'. The battle group had the 2nd and 3rd battalions of the 384th (Croatian) Infantry Regiment. The town of Srb was the closest start point to Drvar, being only some 15 miles (25km) away.

From the north near Bihac (31 miles [50km] from Drvar) 92nd Motorized Regiment with the 54th Mountain Reconnaissance Battalion, supported by

The glider, flown by one pilot, could transport nine passengers in very cramped conditions. The wingspan was 22m. Regular supply flights in the Balkans were conducted and the maximum payload was 1,240kg. Pichler described how there was 'instead of wheels, under the fuselage a type of sled runner made of wide wood, around which barbed wire was simply wrapped, in order to shorten the land area and to brake'. (Slovenian Museum of Contemporary History)

500th SS Parachute Battalion (1,140 men)

Battalion Headquarters	(267)	3rd Parachute Rifle Company	(164)
Signal Platoon	42	Company Headquarters	33
Headquarters Company	66	Signals Section	11
HQ Motor Transport Platoon	30	Parachute Rifle Platoon	40
Section II (Legal)	7	Parachute Rifle Platoon	40
Parachute Maintenance Platoon	31	Parachute Rifle Platoon	40
Supply Company	91	**4th (Heavy Weapons) Company**	**(200)**
1st Parachute Rifle Company	**(164)**	Company Headquarters	33
Company Headquarters	33	Signals Section	11
Signals Section	11	Flamethrower Platoon	28 (2 flamethowers)
Parachute Rifle Platoon	40[1]	81mm Mortar Platoon	34 (4 mortars)
Parachute Rifle Platoon	40	Heavy Machine Gun Platoon	38 (4 machine guns)
Parachute Rifle Platoon	40	75mm Recoilless Rifle Platoon[2]	56 (4 guns)
2nd Parachute Rifle Company	**(164)**	**Training Parachute Rifle Company**	**(181)**
Company Headquarters	33	Company Headquarters	40
Signals Section	11	Signals Section	12
Parachute Rifle Platoon	40	Parachute Rifle Platoon	43
Parachute Rifle Platoon	40	Parachute Rifle Platoon	43
Parachute Rifle Platoon	40	Parachute Rifle Platoon	43

1 *Original source states that each parachute rifle platoon had 39 men, not 40*
2 *One source claims a mixture of 75mm and 105mm guns were available*

The 500th SS Parachute Battalion was larger than a conventional Luftwaffe parachute battalion and possessed its own logistical support. The source for this table is *Forgotten Legions: Obscure Formations of the Waffen SS* by Antonio Munoz.

a regimental group of the 2nd Croat Jäger Brigade, was to drive 'in a southeasterly direction in order to capture Petrovac'. Once there the 92nd 'will then move towards Drvar' in order to 'link up with the SS Parachute Battalion and the Battle Group William'. From the south 1st Brandenburg Regiment and the reconnaissance battalion from 1st Mountain Division were ordered to advance from Knin (40 miles [65km] from Drvar), attack through Bos. Grahovo and make for Drvar. In addition the 105th SS Reconnaissance Battalion by 'driving via Bos. Grahovo towards Drvar, will prevent the escape southwards of the bandit groups, headquarters and military missions'.

Only on 20 May was Rybka told of his battalion's role and assembly areas. Corps orders stated:

SS Para Battalion 500 will drop on D-Day after Stukas have attacked Drvar, with the task of destroying completely and utterly Tito's Main Headquarters. The Commander of our Air Forces in Croatia will order attacks, immediately preceding the landing, upon all identified enemy groups and headquarters, on security areas and anti-aircraft positions. Thereby the enemy will be forced to take cover from the aerial assault. Until D-Day minus 1 the SS Para Battalion will be located as follows. Rybka Group (Parachutists) with headquarters, No. 2 and 3 Companies and a platoon of No. 4 Company in Nagy Betskersk (314 men). The men of No. 4 Company, No. 1 Company, 40 men of the Benesch detachment, 6 men from the Abwehr as well as the Luftwaffe Liaison Troop (320 men) in Zagreb. The second wave of parachutists will be made up of No. 2 Company and the Papa Training Company. This group of 220 men will be located in Banja Luka.

The airborne landing was to commence at 0700. The Germans hoped surprise would enable the paratroopers to swiftly snatch Tito and pin down the partisan forces and headquarters personnel until ground units arrived. An Abwehr contingent (FAT 216 members under Leutnant Zavadil) and Brandenburgers under Leutnant Dowe with Bosnian interpreters would accompany the SS paratroopers and potentially were mission critical. If Tito was not quickly located these specialists were to exploit captured material and personnel to ascertain his whereabouts. A number of army and SS war reporters and photographers were to accompany the mission to record Tito's capture for propaganda purposes.

On the evening of 23 May Rybka drew up his detailed battalion orders. He favoured a glider assault because if flown accurately they could bring in a body of armed men close to the target, achieving maximum surprise with the greatest strength. Despite the efforts to dispatch men quickly from aircraft, paratroops were more dispersed on landing, and had to collect heavy weapons, ammunition and equipment from canisters that had dropped separately.

However, glider units were light on the ground. Up until early 1944 Towing Group 1 with 15 glider tugs and 37 gliders, split into 3 squadrons, was available in the Balkans. 1st and 2nd Squadron each consisted of 17 DFS 230 gliders. 3rd Squadron, stationed in Salonika, was smaller, consisting of three larger Go 242 gliders that were unsuitable for the *Rösselsprung* operation. Towing aircraft consisted of four Henschel 126 for 1st Squadron, six Heinkel 45 biplanes for 2nd Squadron (replaced by Ju-87 dive bombers for *Rösselsprung*) and five Heinkel III for 3rd Squadron.

In February further glider units were brought into the Balkans. 3rd Gruppe from Geschwader 1, comprising 12 Henschel 126 and five Avia towing aircraft, and 17 DFS 230 gliders, arrived from Nancy and on 7 May was transported to Krusevac. In March 1944 2nd Gruppe, consisting of eight Ju-87 dive-bombers used as towing aircraft and eight DFS 230 gliders, arrived in Zagreb from Strasbourg and Mannheim. Despite this reinforcement there were not enough gliders to bring in Rybka's battalion and some of his men would have to land by parachute. However, the situation with air transport aircraft was not much better and Rybka was told that after dropping the first wave transports would have to fly to

6 MAY 1944

von Weichs orders preparation for the *Rösselsprung* operation

Since autumn 1943 1st Squadron of DFS 230 gliders had been operating out of Belgrade and in November was joined by the 2nd Squadron, formed from personnel who had served in the Mediterranean and undergone six months' training that included diving and the use of the brake parachute. In March 1944, when Belgrade became overcrowded, the gliders moved to Samos airfield in the Banat. (Slovenian Museum of Contemporary History)

Banja Luka airfield to pick up a second wave, which could not arrive over Drvar until midday.

In the first wave, 320 men would come in by glider and 314 by parachute. Rybka decided to deploy the parachutists in three main groups, Red (85 men), Green (95 men) and Blue (100 men), to capture and secure the town. With his headquarters staff Rybka would drop with Red group. The troops transported by glider were divided into six groups and each given specific objectives, which had been identified by the intelligence staff, as follows:

Panther Group: 110 men to capture Objective Citadel, presumed to be Tito's headquarters, in the south-western part of town.

Griefer (Attacker) Group: 40 men to capture Objective London, the British Military Mission, 1 mile south-west of town.

Sturmer (Stormer) Group: 50 men to capture Objective Warsaw, the Russian Military Mission, 1 mile north of town.

Brecher (Breaker) Group: 50 men to capture Objective America, the American Military Mission, 1 mile south of town.

Beisser (Biter) Group: 20 men to seize an outpost radio station south-west of town and then assist Griefer.

Draufganger (Daredevil) Group: 50 paratroopers to capture Objective Western Cross, a suspected partisan radio communications centre to the north-west of town. Another 20 men composed of Zavadil's FAT, Brandenburger intelligence officers, Luftwaffe signallers and ethnic German interpreters would join this group.

If Tito was captured a swastika flag would be displayed, if the assault failed a red flare would be fired, the signal for Green parachute group and Sturmer glider group to join Panther for a second attack. Draufganger had the specific mission of questioning detainees and exploiting any information found in the communications centre. The building was near a prominent crossroads and easily recognizable from the air. The second wave of 220 men under the command of Hauptsturmführer Obermeier consisting of the Field Reserve Company and part of 2nd Company, accompanied by two gliders bringing in supplies, were due to arrive over Drvar at 1200. Their chosen landing zone was meadows to the south-west of town.

The location of Tito's headquarters was thought to be a cemetery on a slightly raised position at Slobica Glavica. Aerial photographs had shown a walled position, several anti-aircraft machine guns and an American jeep, which analysts thought indicated the presence of a headquarters. Lieutenant-Colonel Eyre, a Canadian military officer, has opined that the planners of the operation did not use Skorzeny's information, which came from Tetaric and specified the headquarters were located in a cave overlooking the town, because Skorzeny failed to liaise with either Kirchner or Zavadil.

Skorzeny's advice was to cancel *Rösselsprung*. Agents told him that Tito knew the location of his headquarters had been betrayed. Tetaric had indeed been recaptured and on 27 March divulged what he had told the Germans before being shot. Skorzeny was right to presume the partisans expected an

The Ju-52 transport aircraft, used to ferry personnel and supplies, was the workhorse of the Luftwaffe and much in demand in the mountainous Balkans. For airborne operations 12 paratroopers with their arms containers could be carried; however, for *Rösselsprung* only 2nd Gruppe of Transportgeschwader 4 with approximately 40 Ju-52 transport planes had been available. (Bundesarchiv Bild 101I-700-0256-38, Fotograf: Richard Muck)

attack, but whilst Tito fully expected an offensive against Drvar, his chief of staff Jovanovic persuaded him an airborne drop was not likely. However, as a precautionary measure his personal quarters were moved to another cave at Bastasi, 2½ miles west of Drvar, in which he would sleep, returning to his Drvar cave during the day to work. No agents were providing up-to-date information on Tito's whereabouts, he was not being kept under surveillance and this new development was unknown to the Germans. By sheer chance on 24 May Tito decided to stay in Drvar to celebrate his birthday the next day with the Communist Youth League of Yugoslavia, which had just finished its conference. Dedijer, Tito's biographer and fellow partisan, suggested that the Germans were aware of Tito's birthday and deliberately launched a raid on that day, but the German historian Karl-Dieter Wolff dismissed this theory and stated that records pointed to alternative birth dates – Zagreb police had information it was 12 March and the Italian Ministry of Interior 7 May.

Partisan Defences

Drvar, located between the steep Jasenovac Mountains to the north and high wooded hills to the south, was well protected. Although three major roads and a railway led to the town it could only be accessed speedily via a dirt road from Petrovac and approaches were defended by well-fortified positions. The Unac river also shielded the town on three sides and two timber factories and rail yards dominated its eastern side. Luftwaffe bombing raids had forced out most of its population of 1,500, and only 200 civilians remained. Also around the town were communist representatives attending the conference, and personnel from the AVNOJ headquarters and the Central Committee of the Yugoslav Communist Party, perhaps amounting to some 800 people but most of who were lacking in combat experience and had at most the odd rifle and pistol available. An engineering brigade of two weak battalions was also present but the men were mainly labourers who were unused to combat. Prinz Eugen's intelligence officer knew the partisan

Beside Tito is his chief of staff, Jovanovic, who advised a parachute attack on Drvar was unlikely. Jovanovic was a professional army officer of Montenegrin descent. Pro-Russian in outlook, he would be shot in 1947 by border guards whilst trying to flee Yugoslavia after Tito's break with the Soviet Union. (Cody Images)

21 MAY 1944

Rösselsprung given the go-ahead

officer-cadet school was at the nearby village of Sipovljani and Tito's escort battalion of four companies were close by (three companies were present at Drvar, with another at Bastasi). In the wider operational area I, V and VIII Partisan Corps had been identified (six partisan divisions – 12,000 men). I Corps, under Popovic with 1st and 6th Divisions, was closest to Drvar, with corps headquarters in Mokri Nogi, 4 miles down the valley; their nearest formation to Drvar was 3rd Brigade of the 6th Division with four battalions at Kamenica 3 miles away. However, these battalions with approximately 200 men each were nowhere near full strength. V Corps under Slavko Radic was some 10 miles away centred on Petrovac, with 4th Division north-west of Drvar and 39th Division north-east of Drvar. VIII Corps was south-east of Drvar with 9th Division available.

The Allied Missions were all present at Drvar. In February 1944 MacLean had parachuted back into Bosnia with Randolph Churchill, the Prime Minister's son. He carried a letter of support from Winston Churchill that stated the Chetniks would no longer receive arms. MacLean described Drvar as 'a few gutted houses clustered round the gaunt ruins of what had once been a factory' around which 'in a wide green valley, lay open fields with farmhouses and copses'. The British mission 'looked out over the valley onto a range of hills that rose abruptly into a cliff from a river which flowed at its foot'. The American Office of Strategic Services, which conceded Yugoslavia was in the British sphere of influence, viewed MacLean's mission as political and sent an independent intelligence-gathering mission to Drvar. In February a Soviet mission also arrived, by Horsa glider, with General Korneyev (who had been the chief of staff at Stalingrad) and General Gorschkov, a Russian partisan leader, on board; according to MacLean they expected to take charge of the Yugoslav partisan movement. Whilst British and American soldiers acted as military instructors at the partisan officer cadet school, Soviet instructors were lecturing Communist Youth organization members who would become commissars.

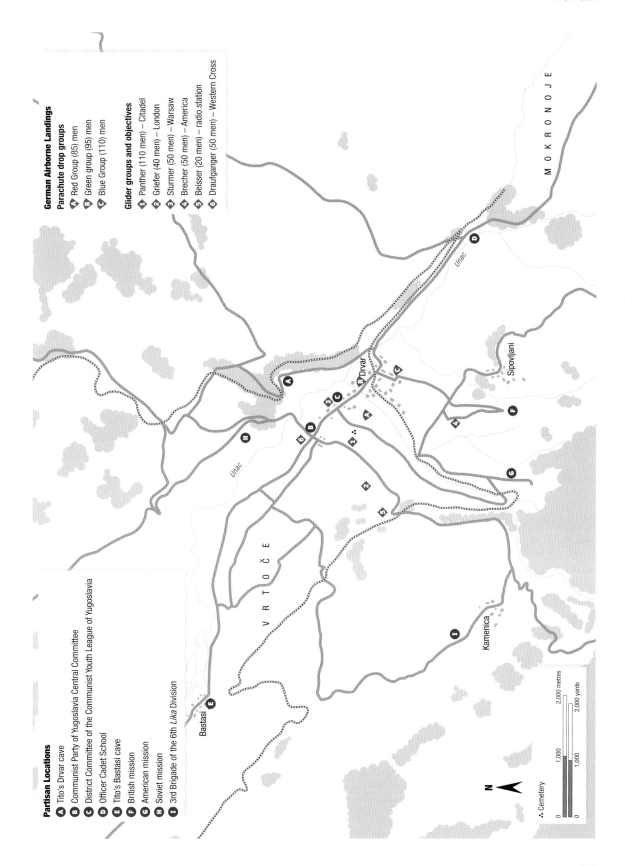

Partisan Locations

Ⓐ Tito's Drvar cave
Ⓑ Communist Party of Yugoslavia Central Committee
Ⓒ District Committee of the Communist Youth League of Yugoslavia
Ⓓ Officer Cadet School
Ⓔ Tito's Bastasi cave
Ⓕ British mission
Ⓖ American mission
Ⓗ Soviet mission
Ⓘ 3rd Brigade of the 6th *Lika* Division

German Airborne Landings
Parachute drop groups

◆ Red Group (85) men
◆ Green group (95) men
◆ Blue Group (110) men

Glider groups and objectives

◆ 1 Panther (110 men) – Citadel
◆ 2 Griefer (40 men) – London
◆ 3 Sturmer (50 men) – Warsaw
◆ 4 Brecher (50 men) – America
◆ 5 Beisser (20 men) – radio station
◆ 6 Draufganger (50 men) – Western Cross

Tito had occupied a house in town but because of the threat of aerial bombardment relocated to a large cave about 60ft above ground, halfway up a cliff face, which had a small waterfall at the back and 'commanded a fine view of the valley'. Tito's biographer, Phyllis Auty, described the headquarters, a 'well nigh impregnable position just outside the town', as follows:

> In a natural cleft in the rock three flights of wooden steps led to a place where the opening widened into a natural cave, inside which rooms had been constructed with a veranda in front commanding a fine view across the valley. Great wooden beams supported the construction and inside in Tito's office the walls were lined, and the windows curtained with parachute silk, while a huge British military map of Yugoslavia covered a wall behind his desk.

In the cave Tito's secretaries Olga and Zdenka were constant companions, as was his friend Kardelj, his intelligence and security officer Rankovic, his two bodyguards and his captured German Alsatian called Tiger.

MacLean became concerned that the increase in the size of the headquarters, which now included the executive and administrative bodies of the new provisional government, and even Zagreb dancers, hampered mobility and security. He felt that the Germans would always be able to concentrate an overwhelming weight of troops and ammunition to force Tito to move. However, some of Tito's advisers suggested digging in at Drvar. Tito asked for supplies – mines, guns, even tanks – to assist a defence. Arguing that partisan forces should retain their mobility, MacLean advised against this approach and advocated keeping the enemy engaged elsewhere. In his memoirs he claimed he had received reports of gliders and troop carriers at Zagreb and wrote how captured documents and intercepts talked of Brandenburgers dressed up as partisans coming to kill Tito. Another plan that came to light was a raid by ski troops from the 1st Mountain Division. German aircraft were often heard and seen flying overhead, sometimes conducting bombing and strafing runs, at other times taking photographs, which gave credence to these concerns.

Tito knew the Germans were preparing an attack on Drvar but misjudged what it would be. A new department called the OZNA acted as a central repository for intelligence and assessed German intentions and dispositions. A translator working for the Ic of 118th Jäger Division reported to OZNA that a German offensive was being planned; however, he did not know the exact place or time. Then on 4 May partisans from the 11th Brigade captured a Chetnik document, which included a map with exact locations for some of the military and political organizations based in Drvar as well as the Allied missions. On 18 May the 39th Division noticed strong movements of troops from Bihac, but falsely assessed their target as Petrovac airfield. Then on 21 May 4th Division observed German forces moving near Knin and Bihac and presumed their target would be Drvar. 6th Brigade even telephoned the duty officer at Drvar and reported that a large number of German aircraft had landed at an auxiliary airfield at Bihac. The warning the duty officer circulated was that all units should expect a heavy aerial bombardment.

Overall defensive measures were limited. At the end of February the 2nd Brigade of 6th Division had been sent to Drvar. Trenches were dug and several camouflaged machine-gun positions were set up. On 28 April the 3rd Brigade replaced the unit; however, on 15 May was itself deployed west to Trubar based on false information of an impending German advance on the town. That left Tito's escort battalion in Drvar, which for immediate defence against aerial attack possessed six AAA guns but the weapons had no sights and often jammed, and four were considered unserviceable.

Tito was aware that a German offensive was likely and with MacLean worked out the priority for airdrops. Many were made around Petrovac and some near Drvar itself or Mokro Nogi. PIAT mortars arrived, which were effective against houses and strong points. Because German aircraft operated relatively freely, partisans were forced to move supplies at night. Flying over Drvar, with its high-sided hills and frequent cloud, was not easy; some aircraft could barely edge into the valley before banking away, which may have led many to discount the threat of an airborne landing. Promisingly there were signs of a growing Allied air presence. Flying Fortresses could be seen flying overhead, then one day their escorting fighters appeared. British SOE/SIS liaison teams, in order to attack targets that partisans had identified, began to call in aircraft from Bari.

In April MacLean was asked to a meeting in Cairo to discuss air supply and took with him a partisan delegate; both were picked up from Petrovac airstrip and command of the British mission was delegated to Vivien Street. On 22 May Street observed a German Fieseler Storch flying at 2,000 feet. It loitered for 30 minutes, flying up and down the valley out of small-arms range. Street warned Tito that an aerial bombardment might soon follow and moved to 'a little house in the hills a mile or two from the town'. The American mission also moved further away. On 23 May Tito gave the opening

Partisans benefited from a windfall of equipment after the Italian surrender in September 1943. Here a small Italian CV-35 tank that mounted a machine gun in a one-man turret is shown in partisan hands. There was a platoon of these tanks at Drvar, which came as a surprise to the paratroopers, and were a danger because of their lack of anti-tank weapons. (Cody Images)

address to the Anti-Fascist Youth conference. The next day, the eve of his 52nd birthday, he sat down with Kardelj in his cave, thinking he was safe from aerial attack below 40–50ft of rock.

Final German Preparations

On 21 May von Weichs submitted the *Rösselsprung* plan to OKW and Hitler gave his official approval. In the evening of 22 May the SS paratroopers, told to be in place by noon on 24 May, began to move to their assembly areas, unaware of the mission that awaited them. Those going to Nagy Betskersk in Hungary with Untersturmführer Hasselwanter drove to Belgrade and then took a train to their destination; those destined for Zagreb with Untersturmführer Witzemann took the railway; and those for Banja Luka with Hauptsturmführer

TITO

Tito was born in 1892 with the name Josip Broz, in Kumrovec, Croatia, close to the Slovenian border. He served a three-year apprenticeship as a mechanic before leaving home at 18 to work all over the Austro-Hungarian Empire. He had a strong sense of family responsibility and sent money home. He believed in the international brotherhood of workers rather than Croatian nationalism and whilst in Zagreb joined the metalworkers' union and Socialist Democratic Party. He loved books and was punished for reading whilst attending machinery. In 1913 he was conscripted and coped easily with the rigours of military service; within a year he was the youngest NCO in his regiment.

In his twenties Tito experienced war, imprisonment and revolution. In the Great War he commanded a reconnaissance platoon on the Eastern Front that raided behind enemy lines to bring back prisoners for questioning. On 25 March 1915 Russian Circassian cavalry caught his regiment in the open and he was wounded in the back whilst fending off another attacker. Taken prisoner, he spent a year in hospital in Russia near Kazan, surviving pneumonia and typhus. He was in charge of a multinational group of prisoners set to work on a railway line in the Urals but when he was discovered altering work records of his colleagues to their advantage, he was beaten by Cossacks. A Bolshevik who tended his wounds told him to go to Petrograd; whilst there he was arrested, questioned in prison, and then put back on a train to the Urals. He escaped and after the Bolshevik Revolution temporarily joined the Red Cossacks in Omsk but when the Whites took the town he took to the steppes with nomadic Khirgiz tribesmen. He was not a committed Red Guard at this time, and found a Russian girl to marry.

In September 1920, with his wife and baby son, he came home to the new kingdom of Serbs, Croats and Slovenes and enrolled in the new Socialist Workers Party. The party was banned on 30 December 1920, despite receiving 12.4 per cent of the vote. After being implicated in bomb plots and political assassinations, severe penalties for communists were announced. However, from 1923 he was an activist and whilst working in the Kraljenica shipyard organized strikes and roused workers through public speaking. By 1927 he was in Belgrade and a full-time Communist party activist. Arrested by the authorities and sentenced, he was bailed on appeal but absconded. In 1928 he took over as Secretary of the Central Committee in Zagreb and distributed arms clandestinely.

Tito learnt the value of trusted associates. He was captured again after being betrayed and was sentenced to five years' imprisonment, a time he spent reading widely and discussing politics with other activists. After his release in 1934 Tito breached a judicial order restricting him to his hometown and again became a wanted man. The police had infiltrated the Communist party and the need for secrecy was paramount. Operating undercover out of Vienna, Tito acted as liaison between the Central Committee of the party, now forced abroad, and party members still in Yugoslavia. He crossed the border numerous times under false identities. The relationship with his wife broke down and he courted a string of mistresses.

Tito's reputation went from strength to strength. In 1936 he organized Yugoslav recruits for the communists fighting in the Spanish Civil War; false names and papers were found for 1,500 volunteers. A new government security drive then pushed him to Moscow, where he was Yugoslav representative on the Communist International (COMINTERN). Surviving the Stalinist purges, upon his

Obermeier also took the Zagreb train, alighting at Nova Gradiska before driving to the airfield. Men wore standard infantry uniforms during transit and concealed their airborne equipment. On 24 May a detailed briefing occurred at Zagreb, which Rybka attended; also present were Chetnik and Ustaše leaders. The plan was distributed along with aerial photographs showing the objectives. Rybka returned to brief his men that evening, for the first time telling them their target.

> The main focus for all sections of the Battalion is Tito's Oberster Stab [headquarters].
> As soon as it is known exactly where the Stab is located, all sections of the Battalion
> who land in close proximity to this chief objective must immediately and ruthlessly

return home he was made Secretary General of the party. He was no ideologue and made practical, rational decisions. The name Tito was a nickname that came from 'that is the problem, this is the solution'. He brought new life into the party, advanced younger members, ended factionalism, widened the recruitment base and brought back the Central Committee from abroad to operate clandestinely.

Tito's earlier experiences building up an underground movement whilst under persistent surveillance served him well during the partisan war. After spending many months with him in the field MacLean identified his attributes: '... leadership, courage, realism, ruthless determination and singleness of purpose, resourcefulness, adaptability and plain common sense. Where there were important decisions to be made ... he took them ... however precarious the situation ... When the partisans were on the move, he moved with them, covering immense distances on horseback or on foot ... he would join the members of his headquarters staff in a convivial meal or a game of chess ... He had the gift, when he chose, of putting his cares aside and relaxing completely. Then he would laugh and joke as if he had not a worry in the world.'

In 1944 partisans sung ballads glorifying him; he had successfully led them through the wilderness for three years and his decisive leadership on the battlefield was credited as saving the movement. In 1943 Churchill told MacLean to 'find out who was killing the most Germans'. Tito's partisans were the answer. Communism gave the partisans in general and Tito in particular a singleness of purpose and ruthless determination, which threatened to unhinge the German position in the Balkans.

In early 1944 Tito was 51 years old and MacLean noticed 'very thin after the rigours of 2 years on the move and long periods of inadequate food'. He was 'clean shaven, with tanned regular features and iron grey hair ... a very firm mouth and alert blue eyes'. His skin 'stretched tight over the bone structure of his face, was parchment coloured from exposure to all weathers'. Beside him is his captured German Alsatian, Tiger. (Cody Images)

At the airfields the packing of parachutes and weapons containers had been carried out that afternoon. By evening 'equipment, ammunition and weapons were checked and the tugs were lined up on the airfield ready for takeoff'. (Tommy Natedal via Marc Rikmenspoel)

eliminate above all the Tito's Oberster Stab. Important persons should preferably fall into our hands living. Written material is to be kept. In the buildings of the Stab fires are to be absolutely avoided, so that men of the intelligence service can come into possession of valuable material.

Rybka concluded by saying: 'Don't waste ammunition, don't stop for the wounded. Press on to the objective.'

Leutnant Sieg, a glider pilot from 2nd Gruppe that would lead the pilots bringing in Panther group, also attended the Zagreb briefing.

On 24 May I drove with my group commander, Captain Jahnke, to Agram [Zagreb] to the Airborne Command Croatia for a briefing on operation *Rösselsprung*. The briefing was attended by almost all participants in the mission, the commanders of the flying units, Hauptsturmführer Rybka, who was to lead SS Paratroop Battalion 500, the leaders of the Chetniks and Ustaše and many others. Under the greatest secrecy the plans of the operation were discussed with reference to aerial photographs.

Pilots were told to land their gliders as close as possible to their targets, even at risk of damage. Sieg then returned to his base where they 'were immediately given precise instructions; likewise the pilots of the glider tugs were informed of the exact flight path, altitude and other operational requirements'.

Relieving forces were moving up to their start lines with elements of the 7th SS Prinz Eugen Division last in place early the following day. At the airfields on the morning of the drop the paratroopers were on parade at 0430. Unterscharführer Pichler with Rybka in Zagreb told how they had been

… accommodated in a school near the airport. No one was permitted to leave or make any contact. None of us, except Witzemann, knew what assignment was before us. We spent one night in the school and were awoken very early around 0400 or 0500 hrs, and the entire Kompanie had to gather in a schoolroom. Here we first learned from our Kompaniechef which mission was flown. From two-tone glasses we could clearly see the aerial photographs of Drvar. On the aerial photographs we saw lines and drawn in points and each group and each Zug [section] was precisely split up over the landing points, direction of attack, etc. While the Schutzen-Kompanien jumped with chutes, primarily the 4. Kompanie was dropped for the most part with transport gliders.

Leutnant Sieg described the events in the early morning.

The men of SS Paratroop Battalion 500 moved to our positions and awaited instructions to embark. A short flight and mission briefing, synchronisation of watches and engines were started. At 05:55 hrs the machines towing the fully loaded transport gliders rumbled ponderously over the ground; the undercarriage was discarded at the end of the field.

Air support for the operation, for 1944, was abundant. Ground-attack aircraft had been specially brought in. On 21 May 1st Gruppe of Stukageschwader 2 had been ordered to move from its airfield near Galatz in Rumania and arrive in Zagreb by 23 May. On 22 May 2nd Gruppe of Jagdgeschwader 51 (20–30 Me 109 fighters) had also been ordered to Zagreb, as was 4th Gruppe of Jagdgeschwader 27 in Hungary, which was told to be there by the evening of 23 May. Airfield Regional Control in Zagreb told Banja Luka airfield to arrange accommodation for 200 men, and Bihac airfield was to ensure bomb craters on its runway were filled in and to provide accommodation for 100 men. All these orders had been intercepted, decoded at Bletchley Park and sent to General Headquarters in Cairo. However, Allied intelligence staffs had not determined the true purpose of *Rösselsprung*. No references to the airborne drop had been made. According to ULTRA historian Ralph Bennett, 'German security had been tight enough to obscure the relationship between the various preparatory measures'. MacLean's biographer, Frank McLynn, believes that there were enough reports to complete the jigsaw but that not one headquarters had them all. He thought, 'a single person in possession of all the material from Yugoslavia reaching Bari and Bletchley would have known the attack was coming. But there was no such person.' ULTRA analysts knew one set of facts, Bari analysts the other. The German airborne attack would achieve its intended surprise.

Leutnant Sieg described how: 'Across the border strongpoint Mokrotz and the Save valley our formation droned, next to us and above us He 46s and CR 42s of Nachtschlachtgruppe 7, the Croatian Luftwaffe Legion with its machines, dive-bomber squadrons and fighter aircraft.' (Michaelis-Verlag Berlin)

THE RAID

Approach and Landing

At 0630, just after dawn, the aerial attack began. Two FW 190 fighters flew up the valley, Tito initially thought 'as if they wanted to prevent the arrival of our Allied aircraft, which had given us so much help', but then 15 Ju-87 Stuka dive-bombers, flying with a squadron of fighters, orbited above Drvar, taking it in turns to plummet earthward and deliver their explosive ordnance on to predetermined targets. Italian-made Caproni 314 medium bombers as well as smaller Heinkel 46 and Fiat Cr 42 ground-attack aircraft also dropped bombs on the town. Leutnant Heinz Schwitzke was a reporter flying in one of the bombers and, in his report filed after the operation, described how 'enormous clouds of dust and smoke were rising from the valley'. And then his aircraft went into the attack: 'We were the last wave of dive bombers to fly right into this dense veil of smoke, which darkened the view from our window, and we threw our bombs into the narrow row of buildings along the street.' For 30 minutes Drvar was pounded from the air, creating a dense smoke that reduced visibility and hampered the identification of landing zones by the approaching glider and Ju-52 pilots.

Parachutists of Blue, Red and Green group were the first to land. Untersturmführer Peter Renold was a communications expert from the Metz Communications School trained by the Waffen-SS at the Forst and Oranienburg radio schools. In mid-May he was one of four members of the school sent to Zagreb, assigned to Zavadil's FAT and given 'strict instructions to use all means to interrupt radio and telephone communications'. He described how 'we landed on a road leading directly to the village ... after we freed ourselves from the harness and armed our weapons, we made our way to our assigned target'. This was the 'Westkreuzes' (Western Cross), where 'German reconnaissance assumed the partisan radio station was located'. However, during the drop losses had been incurred – one parachutist reported how 'in my section there were three missing. Two of them were dead; the third had broken his ankle'.

The gliders soon followed, making their approach from the north-west, many circling twice before making their dive. Leutnant Sieg described how 'shortly before 07:00 hrs we reached the end of the Unac valley flying at an altitude of about 3000 metres. Desperately I searched for Drvar in the morning mist. At exactly 06:50 hrs I released the tow-rope from the machine.' Carrying troops of Panther Group to Objective Citadel he

… decided on a nose-dive with the brake parachute. With a barely perceptible jolt the dive parachute had unfolded at the tail of the fuselage. The heavily loaded glider with its ten occupants lost momentum and dived at a steep angle on the target obscured by smoke and mist. The altimeter dropped at a fast rate, 1500 metres, 1000 metres,

At 0650 Ju-52 transports flying in close formation crossed the 5,000ft mountains, descended to 500ft above the valley floor and slowed to 100 miles per hour. Dispatchers opened side doors and looked out over the town. At 0700 the first paratroopers hurled themselves horizontally into mid-air with arms outstretched. When the canopies opened the parachutists were jerked backwards and their descent took no more than 20 seconds. (Slovenian Museum of Contemporary History)

500 metres and the target, the wall of the citadel of Drvar and the headquarters building, began to take shape. I recognised the two anti-aircraft guns, saw the partisans fleeing in panic and concentrated on the building. As the dive levelled out I attempted to come close to the ground and as near as possible to the wall. Just above the ground I ejected the brake parachute and, as if struck by a whip, my glider shot forward and slid to a halt a few metres in front of the citadel wall of Drvar.

Sturmmann Leo Schapps, a lance corporal in the battalion's signals platoon who had been recruited from the SS Signals Replacement Battalion, was in a glider towed by a Stuka, which set loose its towrope some 4 miles from Drvar. Looking down he saw burning houses and little black dots frantically running about. The steep descent took them from 3,000 to 150ft 'in no time'. The pilot levelled off and then deployed the brake parachute whilst coming in at a 20-degree angle. Partisan fire hit the glider's tail and its left wing clipped a tree 8ft above the ground. The resulting crash resulted in two men taken to the main aid post, with only one man escaping injury free. Schapp's group was fired on after landing, which as a self-confessed 'greenhorn' was a new experience for him.

Leutnant Schuller was an army reporter and described his experiences during the dive.

For Untersturmführer Renold 'the jump from the aircraft went smoothly and without any problems. The time from the opening of the parachute to touch down could not have been more than 12 to 15 seconds. The wind on the ground was suitable for landing.' (Slovenian Museum of Contemporary History)

The pilot calls out: We are plunging down! To me it seems more like a fall, a fast trip in a non-stop lift, rapidly losing altitude. Now the shrillest force of the wind howls through all the gaps … the valley takes shape, the burning village, the flat meadows … Then we crash, and the whole machine shakes so much, that our helmeted heads bump into each other. Somebody shouts: Get out!

Pichler told how 'shortly before landing, on the tail end a braking parachute was cast, which strongly decelerated the steep downward flight. The men sat closely behind each other on a board that was fixed in the middle of the glider and had to push forward with all their power during landing.' (Michaelis-Verlag Berlin)

The descent had taken two to three minutes. Schuller's pilot, 'a very young NCO', was satisfied with his landing and grabbed some grenades 'so that he can carry on as an infantry soldier'. Other gliders were not so lucky and the results of their skidding halt were that 'one of them destroys half of a fruit tree, another slides up the hill, and comes to a stop by its nose, so you can hear how it shatters'.

Shortly after releasing his tow cable, an NCO pilot from 3rd Gruppe carrying troops of Draufganger Group to the Western Cross 'noticed the glider of Oberleutnant Bredenbeck [from Griefer group] which had already lost a lot of height and was most likely crashing'. When his own brake parachute failed to work he managed to pull out of the dive, turn around 180 degrees, and come in again, but then: 'When we landed on the Western Cross the right hand wing strut was snapped off by the force.' However, this did not deter his passengers: 'Before the glider came to a proper standstill, the doors were thrown open and the SS paratroopers were out. While we were landing we came under heavy fire from the eastern mountain slope. No one was wounded and we crept in a flat gully towards the nearest house, where some members of the other glider crews had already taken shelter. The fuel container of the flame-thrower we had brought along was still in my glider, so I rolled back to fetch it.'

Schütze Fritz Hess, an SS private, had also seen the glider with the leader of Griefer Group plummet to the ground. Another had come loose from its towrope and landed at Bastasi, where the company of Tito's escort battalion stationed there killed its occupants. One other glider, from Sturmer group, landed in a field close to Tito's cave and came under intense fire; the rest of the group somewhat fortuitously overshot their target and landed 2 miles away near Vrtoce, despite the pilots flying in loops in an effort to come closer to their objective. Along with Bredenbeck, two further glider pilots – Unteroffizier Schubert and Obergefreiter Kielmann – were killed, both by ground fire whilst landing. In one reported instance the Germans were lucky. Their glider crashed into a boulder, stunning the occupants, and prompted

AIRBORNE ASSAULT ON DRVAR

25 MAY 1944

EVENTS

A   Objective Western Cross, the Communist Party Central Commitee HQ, is successfully assaulted by Draufganger Group.

B   District Committee of the Communist Youth League defends HQ to the last man.

C   Officer Cadets advance to Drvar, and to Tito's cave.

D   Partisan CV-35 tank platoon repulsed by German paratroopers.

E   Hauptsturmführer Rybka establishes command post at cemetery.

F   Most of Sturmer group overshoots target, lands around Vrtoce and has to fight its way into Drvar.

G   In the mid-morning 3rd Bde of 6th Partisan Div approaches Drvar from the Kamenica plateau. Two battalions advance on Rybka's positions and a third swings round to Vrtoce and heads towards Tito's cave.

H   German heavy machine-gun positions established to cover German parachute drop at 1200.

I   From 1030 an assault group advances against Tito's cave but is repulsed by Tito's escort battalion.

J   From 1100 Tito escapes from his cave and ascends to the ridge above.

K   Reinforcing parachute drop at 1200.

L   In the early evening German positions retire to the cemetery and prepare an all-round defence.

M   Partisan reinforcements arrive during the afternoon and evening and advance towards the cemetery.

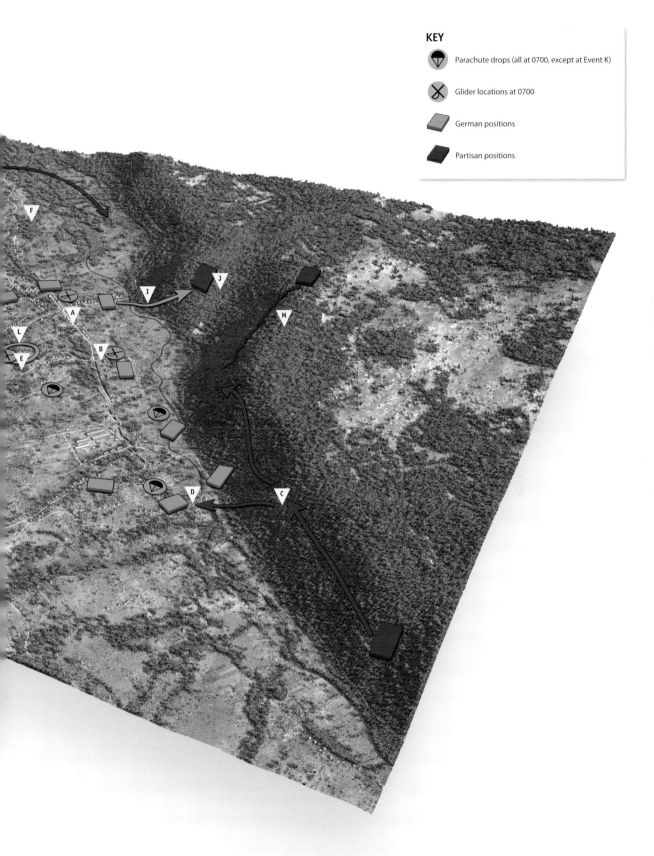

KEY

Parachute drops (all at 0700, except at Event K)

Glider locations at 0700

German positions

Partisan positions

Pichler described how the glider's 'entire fuselage and the wings consisted of light aluminium alloy tube, covered with canvas and camouflage paint'. The passengers, vulnerable to enemy fire during the approach, could quickly disembark after landing. (Michaelis-Verlag Berlin)

some partisans to approach casually, but the Germans came to their senses just in time and shot them all.

Initial Attacks

From gliders that landed safely on target, paratroopers jumped out with their weapons to hand and assaulted their objectives. Despite some initial setbacks the partisans had been taken completely by surprise. Stoyan Pribichevich, a reporter for *Time* magazine, was present at Drvar when the Germans attacked. (Unlike the personnel from the Allied missions, the correspondents had not been moved further away from town.) He described the moment he was told the German attack had begun: 'At 06.30 on the morning of May 25 a Partisan guard woke the British photographer, Slade, the American photographer, Fowler, the British correspondent, Talbot, and me shouting through the windows of our two houses: "Avioni – airplanes!"' The four reached the shelter of a slit trench moments before bombs from an estimated 15 aircraft

Panther group landed close by the cemetery, the suspected location of Tito's headquarters, in part because of the presence of AAA guns. Leutnant Sieg described how 'his group had landed by the citadel with the exception of one glider whose pilot had been hit during the dive'. (Michaelis-Verlag Berlin)

started exploding all around them. Then 'about 30 more, large, low flying planes, arrived and, just as Fowler was filming the dive of a Stuka, brownish parachutes flapped open no more than 200 feet above us and the gliders began to steer towards the ground just in front of us.' The journalists looked at each other and knew there was no escape.

At the cemetery anti-aircraft guns identified by imagery had experienced the full effect of the aerial bombardment and their crews had either been killed or fled. Sieg described how the 'paratroopers stormed over the wall from all sides into Tito's headquarters.' However, more resistance was expected than was encountered and it soon became clear neither Tito nor his headquarters personnel were present. Rybka chose to establish his headquarters here. He was well placed to gain an impression of developments elsewhere. The cemetery was on a hill from which he could see Drvar and nearby valley meadows surrounded by thickly wooded slopes.

Griefer and Brecher Groups failed to find the British and American missions, and the journalists were their only reward. Pribichevich reported how 'a bulky German in a black steel helmet loomed above our trench, pointed his submachine gun at us and yelled "Hända hoch, heraus – Hands up, get out." Pouring out blasphemies, an officer with bulging eyes and thick lips searched us for guns, took away our papers and hit Talbot for not raising his injured right arm high enough.' Immediately the Germans attempted to question prisoners as to Tito's whereabouts and Pribichevich admitted that he inadvertently disclosed his location. When a German produced Tito's photo, Pribichevich 'pointed at the limestone crag beyond the town'. Perhaps realizing his mistake he quickly followed his reply with 'Tito was there last night but he is not there this morning'.

Draufganger Group at the Western Cross experienced the toughest resistance. Here the large building thought to be a communications centre was actually the headquarters of the Central Committee of the Communist Party. Renhold described how 'we found a building into which several land-lines led. There were also several antennae. The building was damaged. As we approached it, a fire-fight developed.' A section of paratroopers dashed

After the impact of landing, section leaders gathered their men to seek out their arms canisters and the paratroopers quickly moved out to secure the eastern and southern approaches to town. (Slovenian Museum of Contemporary History)

forwards and broke down the front door; however, other rooms in the building had been barricaded. Renhold described the enemy as 'partisan officers and armed female communicators in uniform'. When two paratroopers entered through the back door a partisan officer fell to their fire but a female telephone operator who had hidden beneath a desk killed them both before herself succumbing to a grenade blast that sent wooden splinters flying. Partisans in the upper floors continued to resist and the Germans raked the ceiling with fire. Outside a cordon had been established and those seeking to escape through the windows were shot. Satchel charges were used against the strongest barricades and the paratroopers cleared the building room by room with automatic weapons, giving no quarter. Renhold wrote how 'after setting the explosives off and suppressing the resistance, Trupp Savadil could set about its assigned task. Those of us from the Metz junker school reported to Hauptsturmführer Rybka.'

Meanwhile the town was relatively quiet as people sought sanctuary from the bombing. Resistance was sporadic, coming in the main from snipers shooting from houses lining the streets. Such an attack generated an immediate response, from grenades and automatic weapons, which did not distinguish between those that fired the shots and those that were living in the houses. Members of the Communist Youth League still in Drvar contributed to this disparate defence. From a building that housed the district committee of the Communist Youth League, six young men and women refused German demands to surrender and Dedijer described them 'returning German grenades through the window. They fought until the last man fell.' Such fanatical resistance had encouraged the Germans to think Tito may have been there.

Schuller reported how the inhabitants were rounded up for questioning. After 'brief house-to-house fighting, with the usual shots coming from cellars, roofs and church tower windows … Everyone who is still alive, and did not run into the nearby woods when the first bombs fell, is herded together.' He wrote the women 'act totally unreasonably. One of them runs like mad through the vegetable garden. She screams, whilst swinging an Italian gun … She is in a rage, she jumps … then she falls on her face.' Around 400 Yugoslavs were gathered together, many into a large building the partisans used as an administrative office. The Germans were screening as many people as they could to identify those for further questioning, which was being conducted at the battalion headquarters in the cemetery. Zavadil Group, Brandenburgers and attached linguists from the SS Prinz Eugen Division set about determining if any of the detainees knew Tito's whereabouts. All sorts of people had been captured, including Croats and Italians, the Allied newsmen and even American air force weathermen. A district Chetnik commander was released from captivity. From a cellar window a French-Russian medical doctor called out: 'Don't shoot, don't shoot. I German, I doctor.' He tried convincing his captives he had been taken hostage by the partisans. Schuller reported: 'We believe him, at least for now, as he can really bandage a wound.' Paratroopers were also searching for official partisan documents and carried away 'thick paper bundles and folders'.

If Tito was not captured in the initial attack, questioning captured partisans and civilians as to his whereabouts was essential if Rybka was to successfully redirect his forces. Tito knew that most people would have known about his cave but believed that no one in the town told the Germans. The female partisan shown here, called Talic, refused to answer her German interrogators and was taken to Germany after the operation but later escaped. (Slovenian Museum of Contemporary History)

The treatment of captives was unenviable and their fate often subject to chance. Pribichevich described how a soldier with a bandaged head led them 'into the tree-shaded backyard of the two-story Partisan administration building where some 20 old men, women and children had already been herded'. One of two officers present confirmed to the soldier that the journalists should be shot. When Pribichevich declared they were Allied officers the other German officer intervened and they were instead led down into the cellar. Thirty minutes later the soldier returned and 'announced "Engländer und Amerikaner good, aber Partisanen kaput" – indicating that only the Yugoslavs would be executed.' Other prisoners were used to lift and carry, and helped German wounded to the medical aid post at battalion headquarters. Schaap, almost 2 miles away, began to drag his parachute

Accounts vary about who tried to obscure the CV-35 tank driver's vision. Oberscharführer Hummel is cited by Pichler; however, Untersturmführer Waberisch, who had two tank destruction badges earned on the Eastern Front whilst serving with the 3rd SS Totenkopf Division, claimed this was his doing and that Hummel then disabled the tank with a rifle grenade. Here Hummel is pictured in happier times. (Marc Rikmenspoel)

... suddenly two Nietenpanzer, Italian origin – simply taken away from the Italians by the partisans – arrived. Several called for the flamethrowers, but as these wanted to prepare for combat, it became apparent that during landing they were damaged and obsolete. Subsequently, SS Oberscharführer Hummel tore his camouflage combination from his body, ran toward the last tank, jumped up and held the clothing in front of the observation slit so that the driver would not see anything. However, he positioned the tank across the street and jerked back and forth against the house walls and shook off Hummel. Afterwards a man from the tank crew opened the hatch and shot at the man laying on the ground. A graze at the head was the memento of this event. The tanks quickly cleared off and we never saw them again.

Another description of the encounter gives a slightly different version of events. Untersturmführer Waberisch claimed that when one of the tanks was pinning down his platoon and causing quite a few losses, he took off his camouflage smock and with it obscured the driver's vision slit, intending to cause the tank to fall into a trench. When he was wounded and had to jump off, Oberscharführer Hummel then disabled the tank with a rifle grenade and the remaining tanks withdrew. Yugoslav accounts mention how a 16-year-old girl, Mika Bosnic, who was being detained by the Germans, had rushed forward to remove the covering placed over the tank. She was killed but according to Yugoslav accounts her actions enabled the tank driver to make good his escape. After the war the chassis of the tank was retained at the site of a museum outside Tito's cave.

All that had been found of Tito was a new marshal's uniform that was being made for a presentation by the Communist Youth League delegates on his birthday. Rybka's main concern was to ascertain Tito's whereabouts as he needed to act quickly to interdict any escape. However an additional worry was establishing a cordon to guarantee the safety of the drop zone for the second wave. With this in mind at 1000 he sent sections with machine guns towards the base of the heavily wooded ridges to the south-west of Drvar. These men moved through the young wheat fields carrying their heavy weapons and engaged the advancing 3rd Brigade. Mortars and recoilless rifles of the 4th company supported the deployment. Pribichevich wrote he was ordered to carry ammunition for these paratroopers by a burly German sergeant: 'Fifteen paratroopers started out with two heavy machine guns across the young wheatfields toward the wooded, Partisan-held ridge a mile off to the west. To the right and to the left of me similar small groups were advancing in the same direction, some carrying heavy trench mortars.'

During the advance:

... the hail of Partisan bullets gradually grew thicker and we ran across the clear spaces, taking cover from bush to bush, from ditch to ditch, from fence to fence; all the time a German with a submachine gun behind me made sure that I didn't fall out of line. Finally we stopped at an abandoned peasant house on a tree-covered elevation at the very foot of the mountain. Here the Germans set up their two machine guns, made themselves comfortable and ordered me to sit beside one of the guns.

Meanwhile Rybka at the cemetery noticed how resistance was coming from a cliff over the Unac river and realized something important must be over there. He ordered a red flare to be fired, the sign for men from Red, Green and Sturmer Groups to rally on his position for a new assignment. This reorganization took some time and not until 1030 did he send the men he gathered towards the river.

25 MAY
1944

1030
Troops ordered to
move towards
Tito's cave

Attack on Tito's Cave

Tito, in a speech in 1974 to commemorate the 30th anniversary of the Drvar battle, told how he had started to use his cave at Bastasi at night but often came to Drvar to work during the day. He had stayed in Drvar the night of 24 May because the 'next day was my birthday and we wanted to celebrate with the others. On that evening we went to the theatre. We saw a film.' On 25 May he observed that when the Germans found no trace of him in the town the search was widened and was

... furious as I watched them advance across the fields over the Unac towards the cave. Just ten days previously, I told Arso Jovanovic that he had to place machine gun positions along our side of the Unac, just in case the enemy decided to commit paratroopers. Had there been just two or three well entrenched machine-guns, no paratroopers would have been able to cross the river. And so, there were no machine-guns in position. The paratroopers advanced. We shot a few of them. My escort battalion was with me.

When the 'Germans finally realized that there was something here; they began firing into the cave'. Tito described how 'we were able to observe everything from above. No one could leave the cave, except by the streambed.' However, escape from his hut down the track to the Unac valley was too dangerous. Dedijer wrote how 'a courier from Supreme Headquarters went forward to survey the ground and discover the whereabouts of the Germans, but was wounded in the head and fell at Tito's side'. Tito described the incident slightly differently: 'One of our comrades from the escort battalion, a cowardly young man, left and received a bullet through his head.' The Germans had set up a heavy machine gun and it was ranging in on their position.

From Tito's viewpoint the situation was becoming desperate: 'You could see everything, but we were helpless to do anything about it. I took a rifle and began shooting, but someone stopped me.' His entourage consisted of 12 men and eight women. Auty wrote that an escape was 'ingeniously contrived by cutting a hole in the floor of his office [at the mouth of the cave] and dropping a rope to the bed of the stream below'. The historian and

The original German caption reads: 'A paratrooper found a Soviet flag in the accommodation of a Bolshevik commissar.' The partisans shared much in common with their Soviet brethren, including the role of the commissar and political education. Slogans on whitewashed walls were common, particularly the phrase 'Long live Tito, Death to Fascism, Liberty to the People'. (Slovenian Museum of Contemporary History)

former Royal Marine Michael McConville described Tito making use of an emergency exit in his cabin: 'a covered hole that led to a rope placed down the side of a cleft and on to a stream masked by foliage.' A recent biography of Tito by Dr Jože Pirjevec quotes a member of Tito's escort battalion who tells how Tito thought the game was up and, seeing the Germans advance towards the cave, put on his marshal's uniform so he could be identified properly. He had to be persuaded by Rankovic that escape was still possible and practically at gunpoint was told to climb down the rope. Pirjevec also quotes the young partisan describing how his comrade who had been shot in front of the hut was only wounded and because his screams were giving Tito's position away he was dispatched with a pistol. Needless to say neither Tito nor any of the senior leadership mentioned this version of events.

Once down the rope the Unac valley floor was no safe place to be. Kardelj apparently had a narrow escape when 'the Germans passed within feet of his hiding place'. Rankovic's plan was now to climb up the cleft in the rock to the ridge above, using a previously laid rope ladder that had been set out for such an eventuality. Tito told how this ascent was made from the streambed, referring to how only the noise of his dog had prompted thoughts of using his pistol: 'I left with the help of my escort and my dog, Tiger. After we climbed for a while, I had to take a rest. Tiger came to me. He started to whine. I grabbed him by the snout to keep him quiet. There were times that

I thought we would have to shoot him with a pistol, because he would betray us, but I couldn't bring myself to do it.' With no further incident the group ascended up the ridge. Tito was still reluctant, thinking that the Germans would have surely landed some men on the top of the ridge who would be waiting in ambush for them.

Emerging on to the plateau Tito was relieved to find a group of partisans. Even then he described how 'the Germans noticed us and began shooting their machine-guns at us. Thank God, no one was hit', and then 'aircraft returned and began to bomb the area around the cave. The entire mountain appeared to shake.' Schuller mentioned how German warplanes circled the valley at midday and threw 'their bombs into the rock crevices and bomb the area with their weapons'. German air support was only possible after the attack had been broken off for fear of hitting their own soldiers. Tito's party had a narrow escape and split into small groups to make their way eastwards to Potoci, 10 miles distant.

Renhold described the attack on the cave entrance from the German perspective. Whilst the river may not have been covered by machine guns he wrote how the cave was 'secured by five guard posts armed with machine-pistols. Three of them were located right in front of the cave, while the other two were in front of the building in which members of the escort battalion slept.' He estimated that 100 men were guarding the cave and described how 'the fighting was fierce and conducted without compromise. The wounded were disarmed and left lying. We also suffered many losses and wounded who could not immediately be treated.' Jovanovic, Tito's chief of staff, had rallied the escort battalion and led the unit in the defence of the cave. Renhold also mentioned how partisan officer cadets who had crossed the

Renhold described how 'Group Obermeier landed in the valley and suffered heavy casualties'. He dismissed their impact on the operation and by midday described the battalion's situation as critical. Most of the reinforcements joined those troops holding the perimeter to the west of town. (Slovenian Museum of Contemporary History)

river to the north bank of the Unac also 'diverted us from the main headquarters by their flanking attack'.

Reinforcement and Regrouping

Rybka had not been able to commit enough paratroopers to the attack on the cave. At midday, whilst Tito was climbing up to the plateau, Ju-52s returned with reinforcements – 220 SS paratroopers under Hauptsturmführer Obermeier that dropped on to the fields to the south-west of town. However, it is difficult to conceive what role these men were going to have here. After Rybka realized the ridge was Tito's hiding place, committing these men to land on top of this feature, which was clear of trees, would have been the better decision. Rybka, because there were not enough transports or gliders to take his battalion in one wave, unexpectedly had a company in reserve, which was available to drop where he chose fit. However, during the planning stage it seems that no alternative landing zones had been prepared and that a change in the second wave's landing zone was not envisaged.

If dropped on the treeless plateau above Tito's cave, Obermeier's men could have interdicted Tito's escape route. According to Schapp, Rybka had a 20-watt transmitter that had successfully established communications with a reconnaissance aircraft flying above Drvar, which relayed messages back to Zagreb airfield. He could have informed them of a change in plan. However, Schaap stated that the 80-watt transmitter for communicating with 2nd Panzer Army Headquarters in Kragujevac was not working well. Perhaps Rybka was hesitant about changing the plan without authorization from higher headquarters. Alternatively, perhaps during the rushed planning stage he believed too confidently in the fidelity of the intelligence that located Tito in the cemetery to the west of the town and could not conceive an alternative landing zone for the second wave might be necessary once the operation was launched.

In the early afternoon Rybka organized a second, by then futile attack on Tito's cave, which also came to grief. Elsewhere the machine-gun positions that Pribichevich had helped establish in the meadows to the west of Drvar were holding, despite increasing partisan fire. He wrote how 'by 2 pm the firing rose in a steady crescendo from all sides. Partisan bullets and grenades tore viciously through the bushes and tree branches around me. The two German machine guns rattled incessantly against the hillside.' A farmer and his son were also helping. The father was wounded in the arm and bandaged. 'The terrified boy, trembling like a leaf, wrung his hands, whimpered and implored the Germans in Serbo-Croatian, "I want to go home, I want to go home." The Germans ignored him and soon a Partisan machine-gun burst shattered both his knees. The Germans did not bother trying to bandage him.'

German and Croatian aircraft were active during the day but distinguishing friend from foe was difficult. Pribichevich witnessed how 'a dozen dive bombers droned overhead, but their bombing soon had to be stopped for fear of hitting the Germans'. At 1500 Rybka radioed a message to 2nd Panzer Army regarding the situation of his battalion: 'Are completely

OPPOSITE
Tito looks down from the veranda of the hut that is located at the mouth of the cave he is using as his personal quarters. It is about 60ft above ground and half way up a cliff face. He is horrified to see German paratroopers advancing across the river Unac towards his position. A partisan guard has been hit by heavy machine gun fire that is supporting the German assault. Behind Tito Rankovic, his intelligence chief persuades him to return inside the hut to make use of an emergency trap door.

25 MAY 1944

midday 220 SS paratroopers reinforce Rybka's force

Signallers from the 500th SS Parachute Battalion are shown here at Drvar. Leo Schaap claimed his colleague Bastian was having trouble exchanging call signs with radio operators from the 2nd Panzer Army at Kragujevac. (Michaelis-Verlag Berlin)

open to enemy view. Injured cannot be cared for properly. Enemy is amassing strong forces.' Schuller described how 'more and more bullets are raining down from the mountain slopes into the valley. Every single soldier comes under fire from snipers, who are hiding amongst the bushes and trees. It is a dreadful feeling.' The paratroopers were suffering from thirst. One veteran recounted how 'in the heat of the afternoon we would have sold our souls for a cool drink. We had all taken the pep pills before take-off, to give us extra energy and faster reflexes. We all knew that the tablets had unpleasant side effects but we thought that we would be able to withstand the raging thirst that they produced. It was a real torment.' This was the least of their worries as more partisans from the 6th Proletarian Division began to arrive.

Relief Force Stalled

The drop of the 500th SS Parachute Battalion on Drvar was only one – albeit potentially critical – part of the XV Mountain Corps offensive. The forces coming to the assistance of the battalion were also ideally positioned to encircle substantial partisan formations and if Tito escaped, the airborne assault could intercept him too. These follow-on operations were integral to German expectations for *Rösselsprung*. The Brandenburgers were involved in providing follow-up targeting. On 24 May Benesch sent a request to Fliegerführer [Air Force Commander] Croatia proposing a bombing raid for 26 May on a building a mile or so from Potoci railway station, some 15 miles east of Drvar, which he identified as one of Tito's emergency headquarters. For the operation he suggested using Major Blaich, who had flown missions for the Abwehr in Africa.

For the wider offensive the terrain benefited the defender rather than the attacker. The area of operations was bounded by the Una river to the west and the Vrbas river to the east and consisted of a series of wooded hills penetrated by few roads. On the western side the Unac river flowed north-west into the Una some miles south of Bihac. On the eastern side the Sana river flowed parallel to the Vrbas a few miles to its west and along its eastern bank partisan positions were well established.

The units of the SS Prinz Eugen Division had been tasked with breaking through the Sana positions and advancing towards Drvar to unite with elements of the 373rd (Croatian) Infantry Division coming in from the west, and the 92nd Motorized Regiment with supporting Croat formations and 54th Mountain Reconnaissance Battalion advancing from the north. In the south the 1st Brandenburg Regiment with the 1st Mountain Division's Reconnaissance Battalion were advancing north to Drvar and the 105th SS Reconnaissance Battalion and 369th Reconnaissance Battalion were tasked with stopping partisans from breaking out. Many sub-units from a variety of different units were assigned to the XV Mountain Corps and coordinating them would be a challenge.

Confidence must have been high within the SS Prinz Eugen Division. The formation was conceivably the most experienced at anti-partisan operations and the divisional order stated 'combat effectiveness of the red formations is limited'. However some trouble with moving units was expected as the order also told how 'roads and bridges on the periphery of the occupied area are mined or destroyed'. The division committed all three battalions of the 13th SS Mountain Regiment, the 7th SS Reconnaissance Battalion, and a company of the 7th SS Engineer Battalion. These units had some distance to travel before reaching their assembly areas, with one battalion transported overnight by train from Bugojno to Jajce (on the Vrbas). Motor transport was then provided to take them forward to their start lines to the south-west of the town and had to return to bring another battalion forward. The 3rd Battalion and the divisional reconnaissance battalion assembled further west at Mrkonjicgrad. Further back and to the north a *panzergrenadier* battalion from the 2nd Panzer Army reserve – comprised of officer cadets – and the 202nd Panzer Company, both attached to Prinz Eugen for the offensive, formed up at Banja Luka. While it was unlikely that any of the German units approaching Drvar from the east would reach the town on 25 May, their subsequent successful advance could intercept any retreat Tito sought to make in that direction, if he survived the airborne assault.

On 25 May Brigadeführer Kumm described how 'concentrated attacks by all battle groups ran into prepared enemy positions. They offered stiff resistance and, in some places, counterattacks.' The next day enemy resistance 'stiffened'. The road between Mrkonjicgrad and Mliniste became blocked from the Srbina pass and a Cossack engineer battalion was deployed to clear the way. Only that night did the partisans – comprising elite units of the 1st Proletarian Division – start withdrawing to the west. The 3rd Battalion of the 13th SS Mountain Regiment moved south-west down the Mliniste road in an attempt to outflank the retreat of those partisans facing the 1st and 2nd battalions. The *panzergrenadier* battalion had made quicker progress. After removing a series of roadblocks their advance reached Kljuc on the Sana river on 27 May, but a bridge had been destroyed there and would not be

Partisan Forces at Drvar

Official Bodies in Drvar
Supreme Headquarters
Anti-Fascist Council of the National Liberation of Yugoslavia
The Central Committee of the Communist Party of Yugoslavia
The Central Committee of the Communist Youth League of Yugoslavia
The District Committee of the Communist Youth League of Yugoslavia
Communist Youth League Delegates
Allied Missions (UK, US, USSR)

Formed Units – Start	
Engineer Brigade, 2 battalions	400 approx.
1st, 3rd & 4th companies, escort battalion	250

Reinforcing Units – Early morning	
Officers' school cadets	130
CV-35 tank platoon	3 tanks

Reinforcing Units – Mid-morning	
1st, 2nd & 3rd battalions, 3rd Brigade, 6th Lika Division	600

Reinforcing Units – Mid-afternoon	
4th Battalion, 3rd Brigade, 6th Lika Division	200
2nd Company, escort battalion	100

Reinforcing Units – Evening	
1st Battalion, 1st Brigade, 9th Dalmatian Division	300 approx.
1st Battalion, 1st Brigade, 6th Lika Division	300 approx.

Formed units in Drvar were initially few; however, reinforcements arrived throughout the day. Many official bodies were present in or immediately around Drvar, perhaps amounting to some 800 people, but most would have lacked combat experience and been poorly armed.

repaired until late the next morning. A partisan ambush in their rear, some 8 miles south-west of Banja Luka, also disrupted their further advance.

In the south-west the 1st Brandenburg Regiment on the march from Knin in the direction of Grahovo soon ran into trouble. Partisan positions on the mountaintops of Sator and Jadovnik north-east of Grahovo were assaulted by the 2nd and 3rd Battalions with artillery support, but the partisans were themselves supported by Italian artillery pieces and held their positions throughout the day. The regimental commander sent reinforcements to this sector and gathered forces for a decisive attack the next day but the partisans evacuated the position overnight. The 105th SS Reconnaissance Battalion made better progress, though at 1800 on 26 May the unit was still 6 miles south of Drvar. No relief force would come to the paratroopers' assistance from the east or south. The paratroopers would have to rely on the attacks of the closest units to them – the 92nd Motorized Regiment and the 373rd Infantry – from the north and west.

Fight for Survival

During the late afternoon Rybka was wounded by grenade fragments. Renhold wrote how 'we drove a wedge into the enemy with a small group, so that we could recover our commander'. The second in command Hauptsturmführer Obermeier had also been wounded and was cut off from the rest of the battalion. According to Schaap, the wounded Rybka advised Untersturmführer Haselwanter to break out, and the remaining company commanders all agreed. The battalion adjutant Obersturmführer Mertley demurred and advocated an all-round defence of the cemetery. He was then also wounded and Hauptmann Bentrup, a Luftwaffe officer commanding the glider pilots, took charge of the battalion because he was the most senior officer remaining and issued new orders to retreat to the cemetery.

By 1900 partisan mortars were targeting the cemetery. A direct hit destroyed the radio and broke all contact with higher headquarters. Schuller probably was not exaggerating when he wrote 'from all sides new guerrilla groups seep into the woods – one can't see them, but one can feel it and it shows by the gradually increasing firing power. We are fired upon incessantly and the shots hit the gravestones, deflected bullets ricochet above our heads. Now we can only move forwards on our stomachs.'

Pribichevich was still with the German machine-gun groups in the meadows and described how these positions were in danger of becoming isolated. At 1800 'to the right, at the end of the valley, on a gentle hill with a bombed church outlined against the glowing horizon, a single file of men appeared, marching toward the German rear'. By 1900 the route back to headquarters – a mile away – was under fire. By 2030 when the retreat was ordered, 'dusk was falling and tracer bullets raced over the Drvar Valley like fireflies'.

Pribichevich described the desperate withdrawal. He made for a hedge and could see a shallow ditch beyond, between two wheat fields, which led back toward the cemetery. He thought a partisan sharpshooter was firing at him and, carrying a wounded German on his back, staggered as quickly as he could with his burden. He wrote he had 'no recollection of how I crossed

26 MAY 1944

0030 Final partisan attack on cemetery beaten off

Here a German LMG provides covering fire from outside Drvar church. Partisan pressure was mounting on German paratroopers in the town and towards evening there was a danger isolated groups would be cut off. (Slovenian Museum of Contemporary History)

those 30 yards except that I made the ditch and dropped on all fours with the wounded German riding my back'. Other German soldiers behind him were 'running one by one across the clear space and jumping over the hedge into the ditch behind me'.

He decided his best chance was to 'pretend to be retreating, but actually to drop behind and let the Partisans catch up with me'. When he started to shuffle slowly on his knees and elbows 'the wounded man on top of me groaned, got off me with an agonizing effort and stumbled away into the gathering darkness. A few more Germans overtook me while Partisan bullets grazed the edges of the ditch. I pushed myself forward on my stomach and I saw a couple of Germans trying to run over a clear space and turning somersaults as the machine-gun burst hit them.' A sergeant shouted after him but after 'a few more sham efforts at scuttling ahead I stopped again and looked back. There was not a single living German behind me.' Soon afterwards 'scores of battle-crazed Partisans came bounding across the wheatfield, brandishing their fearful hand grenades'. He was able to surrender in Serbo-Croat, which probably saved his life.

Not all the paratroopers had received the order to gather at the cemetery. One group, cut off and surrounded in the early evening, was eventually overwhelmed with no survivors. However, the paratroopers from Schafer's group in the weather station were told of the withdrawal and set off for the battalion headquarters. Once there they formed a rearguard to hold back the partisan pursuit.

… our Granatwerfer [mortar] were set up in front of the cemetery, which plastered the following partisans … I set up an MG in front of the Granatwerfer position and for a long time held the advancing partisans at a proper distance until an MG-Schutze [machine-gunner] fell from a direct hit from a Granatwerfer – I got off with a fragment in the neck. Subsequently we were the last to pull back into the cemetery. The night was illuminated from the tracer ammunition.

The cemetery was approximately 250 feet by 164 feet. Around 700 men occupied this area, including 150 with serious wounds. Determined partisan attacks were expected with the coming of darkness. (Slovenian Museum of Contemporary History)

60

The NCO glider pilot that had landed at the Western Cross was also retreating and made it back to

> … a flat trench dug along the north-western edge of the cemetery uninjured, where the men were already sheltering shoulder to shoulder. A few metres behind me a radio post had been set up and on the south-western end of the citadel there was a collecting point for the wounded.

As supplies of ammunition were running low 'small groups tried, without success, to reach the damaged transport gliders and carry off as many weapons as possible, such as MG 42s, ammunition and other supplies'.

With the oncoming darkness Schuller wrote how 'on they will come. And they do. Full of rage and desperation … Everyone has dug himself into a hole, as deeply as possible.' The dark made 'the tall grasses and cornfields, as well as the trees and shrubs, look blurred, and the surging merciless attacks make it a night of hell. The constant hammering of the mortars and the bullets of the infantry is horrifying.' Sieg confirmed how 'at times the fire simply hailed down upon us'. Once the paratroopers suspected that partisans were attempting to infiltrate men close to the cemetery illumination flares were fired. However, the partisans used the dark to envelop the cemetery and by 2200 grenades started to come over the north wall.

During the night the 1st Battalion, 1st Brigade, 9th Dalmatian Division, and 1st Battalion, 1st Brigade, 6th Lika Division arrived, but it was the 3rd Brigade from the 6th Lika Division that was still at the forefront of the attacks with its 4th Battalion in the lead. An SS war reporter, Adalbert Callewart, described how

> … at the onset of darkness the bandits advance again. They approach from all sides … the bullets whistle from every direction over the heads of the Fallschirmjäger … nothing can be seen of the desolate mountain ridges that surround the valleys any longer. Sometimes everything is calm and no shots interrupt the silence. Suddenly the machine guns rattle from all sides and from every corner, and the impact of heavy grenades stir up the defender's position.

The number of wounded mounted but those still capable would 'fill the magazine for the sub machine guns and prepare the munitions belt for the machine guns'.

The German defence was organized into an outer perimeter of positions and a smaller inner perimeter. After every partisan attack the men in the outer perimeter were relieved. One paratrooper described what happened when partisans were seen climbing over the wall at 0130.

> … a whole mass of flares burst – all of them white – and in the glare the bandits were silhouetted. We shot them down, but they seemed to be immune to rifle fire and kept coming. Then some of them from behind cover of the wall threw hand grenades and got some light mortars into action. In that particular attack, the Reds actually got inside

OVERLEAF
In the early evening the remnants of the battalion have retreated to the cemetery south-west of town, which was on a slight rise surrounded by valley meadows and thickly wooded slopes. The SS paratroopers are using a raised bank of earth as rudimentary cover. In the foreground a German gunner has been firing his MG 42 so much his barrel has overheated and he is in the process of changing it, offering a temporary lull for the partisans to climb the wall and gain access to the cemetery to engage the defenders in close-quarter battle.

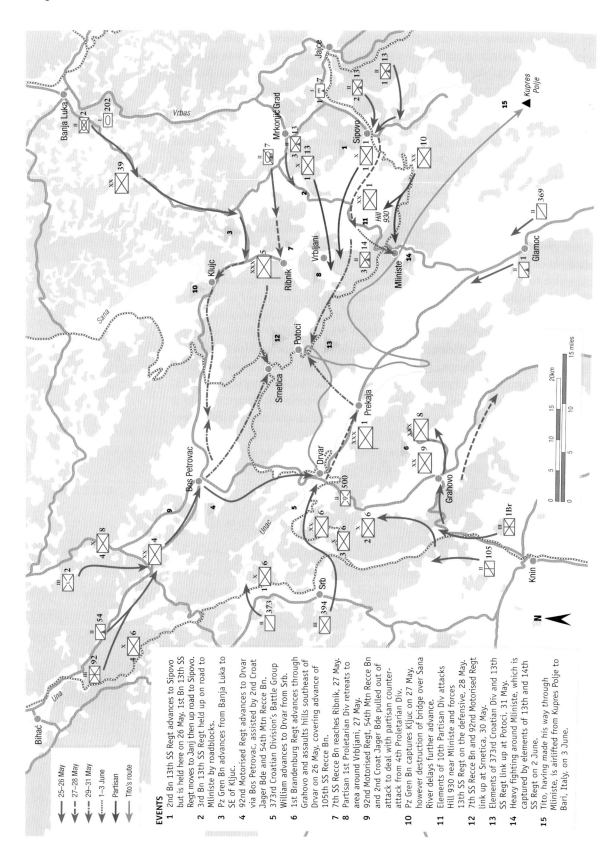

EVENTS

1 2nd Bn 13th SS Regt advances to Sipovo but is held here on 26 May. 1st Bn 13th SS Regt moves to Janj then up road to Sipovo.

2 3rd Bn 13th SS Regt held up on road to Mliniste by roadblocks.

3 Pz Gren Bn advances from Banja Luka to SE of Kljuc.

4 92nd Motorised Regt advances to Drvar via Bos Petrovac, assisted by 2nd Croat Jager Bde and 54th Mtn Recce Bn.

5 373rd Croatian Division's Battle Group William advances to Drvar from Srb.

6 1st Brandenburg Regt advances through Grahovo and assaults hills southeast of Drvar on 26 May, covering advance of 105th SS Recce Bn.

7 7th SS Recce Bn reaches Ribnik, 27 May.

8 Partisan 1st Proletarian Div retreats to area around Vrbljani, 27 May.

9 92nd Motorised Regt, 54th Mtn Recce Bn and 2nd Croat Jager Bde pulled out of attack to deal with partisan counter-attack from 4th Proletarian Div.

10 Pz Gren Bn captures Kljuc on 27 May, however destruction of bridge over Sana River delays further advance.

11 Elements of 10th Partisan Div attacks Hill 930 near Mliniste and forces 13th SS Regt on the defensive, 28 May.

12 7th SS Recce Bn and 92nd Motorised Regt link up at Srnetica, 30 May.

13 Elements of 373rd Croatian Div and 13th SS Regt link up at Potoci, 31 May.

14 Heavy fighting around Mliniste, which is captured by elements of 13th and 14th SS Regt on 2 June.

15 Tito, having made his way through Mliniste, is airlifted from Kupres Polje to Bari, Italy, on 3 June.

25–26 May
27–28 May
29–31 May
1–3 June
Partisan
Tito's route

45 aircraft on the ground and damaging 96 other, [and] virtually eliminating the GAF [German Air Force] as a combat force in Yugoslavia'.

Less effective was an amphibious diversion launched from Vis: 2,500 partisans and 900 Royal Marines landed on the island of Brac. German defensive preparations included covered trenches and mines on the 2,000ft hill that dominated the island. The attack, by elements of 40 and 43 Commando, stalled under heavy fire and 127 casualties were suffered. The Germans reinforced the island with an extra 1,900 men, but these troops were not taken from the forces around Drvar.

The Germans would be able to interdict Tito's escape if partisan defences on the eastern side of the cordon collapsed. On 27 May positions opposite the 1st and 2nd battalion of the 13th SS Mountain Regiment were evacuated. The 7th SS Reconnaissance Battalion advanced westwards and reached Ribnik. (Prisoner-of-war statements falsely located Tito here.) However, German pressure from the north abated when the 92nd Motorized Regiment, and its accompanying reconnaissance battalion and Croat brigade at Petrovac, were temporarily withdrawn for two days to attack the 4th Partisan Division of V Corps that had started a diversionary attack. The next day the partisans also launched another counterattack against the SS Prinz Eugen Division. The 10th Partisan Division from VIII Corps attacked Hill 930, which was 3 miles north-east of Mliniste, from the south-east. Tito was passing through the town on his way to Kupres and spoke after the war how as they passed Mliniste 'mortar rounds were falling right onto the road we had to take … A round fell directly behind me and wounded a Russian. Then the entire detachment quickly ran across the road. There were no losses. Only two comrades were wounded.' Avoiding a sniper's hut the group set up camp in the woods and the next day continued on their journey.

Kumm wrote the partisan counter-attack caused the division command post to end up between the lines. The headquarters guard company and communications personnel had to be committed to rescue the situation. However, by 29 May 'large enemy columns were observed withdrawing' as the partisans completed their withdrawal west of the Sana. Indicative of how the operation was reaching its apogee, 2nd Panzer Army signalled XV Mountain Corps 'the chances of success depend upon speed of manoeuvre' and ordered 'all battle groups must report at least once every four hours'.

In Tito's group Captain Hilary King, the British signals officer, had the only working radio and he called in supplies by air, including 'several machine-pistols and some ammunition'. Tito was on the run and unable to exert any influence on partisan operations. He thought he could evade capture indefinitely in the Bosnian woods, but did concede he could not direct the war from here. King's radio was used to report Tito's predicament to Bari. Korneyev, having lost a leg at Stalingrad, was finding the cross-country march difficult and suggested evacuation by air. Rankovic wanted to make the move permanent. Initially Tito was reluctant to leave because he feared the consequences such a move might have on partisan morale. He had an argument with Korneyev and told how 'the Englishman, Street took his [Korneyev's] side'.

3 JUNE 1944

Tito evacuated to Italy

6 JUNE 1944

Operation *Rösselsprung* terminated

On 29 May, on the western side of the cordon, Battle Group William's advance ran into strong resistance around Prekaja and stalled because of a lack of ammunition. According to Kumm the partisans could fight determinedly because 'the terrain allowed them to withdraw unnoticed'. Further north on 30 May the 3rd Battalion of the 92nd Motorized Regiment finally made contact with the 7th SS Reconnaissance Battalion at Srnetica railroad station. However the aim of pursuing Tito was seemingly losing out to the encirclement and destruction of the partisans. On 31 May, after 373rd (Croatian) Division broke through in the Prekaja area and met up with Prinz Eugen at Uvala and Potoci, a new corps order was issued that stated 'the enemy in the Unac-Sana forest region will be destroyed'. Despite realizing that the main body of the enemy was withdrawing to the south, west and south-east, Leyser wanted to concentrate on the partisans that had not escaped rather than pursue those that had.

In fairness there had been problems maintaining the pursuit. The 92nd Motorized Regiment, criticised by Kumm for not wanting to deploy off the main roads, was committed to securing supply routes. To give the Prinz Eugen more impetus, a battalion from the 14th SS Mountain Regiment was brought in to replace 2nd Panzer Army's *panzergrenadier* battalion. Allied air power was making an impact, Kumm reported that 'several deep air attacks' had occurred on the Kjluc–Mrkonjicgard road and Allied aircraft were also dropping supplies to the partisans. On the road from Mrkonjicgrad to Mliniste 20 new obstacles had been placed, which helped stall the German advance and enabled Tito's march to continue without interference. The

Here photographed as a Standartenführer, from January 1944 Brigadeführer Kumm was the commander of the 7th SS Prinz Eugen Division, which in 1942 had been recruited from ethnic Germans living in Yugoslavia. A historian of Tito's partisans, Velmir Vuksic, wrote 'almost all Partisans agreed that their most dangerous opponents were the 7th SS Prinz Eugen' and 'tried to avoid engaging it whenever possible'.

13th SS Mountain Regiment turned to destroying partisan facilities and supply dumps in the Potoci–Uvala area. On 3 June the Germans formally halted the pursuit and ordered units to comb their immediate areas. Developments in the south, which needed to be successful to block retreating partisans, were not going well – the 105th SS Reconnaissance Battalion and the 369th Reconnaissance Battalion were ordered to clear their own areas, rather than prosecute further attacks.

After three days – during which time the German offensive had gained momentum but coincidentally when orders had been issued for its termination – Tito eventually conceded to an evacuation, providing he could establish his headquarters on Vis. On the night of 3 June Shornikov, a Soviet fighter ace, landed a Dakota on an airstrip at Kupresko Polje and took Tito to Bari in southern Italy. (From May 1944 as part of an Allied agreement Russian pilots had begun flying American aircraft from Bari, a British-run airfield). Another six Dakotas landed in quick succession and took off another 74 personnel from his staff and the Allied missions, and 118 wounded partisans. Tito spent two nights in Bari before boarding the British destroyer HMS *Blackmore*, now accompanied by Fitzroy

MacLean, for Vis. After a convivial dinner in the wardroom Tito sang 'The Owl and the Pussycat' in English to the assembled officers. Once on the island he established a new headquarters in a mountain cave. The 'most dangerous enemy' was back in control. SOE came up with a plan to deceive the Germans into thinking he was still in Yugoslavia. Radio traffic from the Croatian partisan headquarters could be worded to suggest Tito was there. However whilst Tito and MacLean approved the plan, Gosnjak, the partisan leader in Croatia, was less keen, expecting the Germans would soon triangulate the position of the broadcaster and launch another attack on his location. The plan was dropped.

The Allies need not have worried about deceiving the Germans. Fearing the game was up, and with the news of the Allied landing on the beaches of Normandy, the Germans announced the termination of *Rösselsprung* on 6 June. That day Prinz Eugen units were re-subordinated to V SS Mountain Corps and ordered to move back through Mrkonjicgrad and Jajce. The Germans were forced to measure success in terms of enemy casualties and military supplies captured, and in these terms declared the offensive a resounding triumph. The 2nd Panzer Army reported the operation had destroyed the core region of the partisans by 'occupying their command and control and their supply installations' and 'forcing the elite communist formations … to give battle and severely battering them'. OKW reported 'the enemy lost 6,240 men'. XV Mountain Corps reported 1,916 partisans killed, with only 161 listed as captured and a further 35 counted as defectors. German losses were announced as 213 soldiers killed, 881 wounded and 57 missing – a total way below the true figure.

When the battalion's vehicles arrived at Drvar the paratroopers could commence their withdrawal. First 50–60 captured partisans had to be escorted to Petrovac. One paratrooper described how this took several days because 'we were attacked several times by American four-engined Bombers and Jabos [Allied fighter bombers] … All movement had to be carried out at night in this region because during the day when we were marching, the Jabos were already there.' He assumed that 'the Americans were informed of our movements from the partisans via radio'. The next leg of the journey from Petrovac to Bihac was still through partisan territory and the paratroopers were on high alert. During a short break 'we received fire from the right and then also from the left of the street. After the entire battalion was completely ready for combat, fire was returned from all infantry weapons … Except for a few lightly wounded we had no casualties.' The motorized column continued on its way and in mid-June arrived in Ljubljana where the remnants of the battalion had a period of rest and reorganization.

AFTERMATH

By the end of June the 500th SS Parachute Battalion, with its new commander SS Hauptsturmführer Siegfried Milius, mustered 292 men fit for duty (15 officers, 81 NCOs and 196 enlisted men). Tito's presence on Vis became known but such was the strength of the defences a German plan to drop paratroopers on the island, including the remnants of the battalion, was abandoned – Dedijer suggested because of the confusion following the attempt on Hitler's life on 20 July. The unit instead entrained for the Baltic and prepared for a drop on the Finnish Aland Islands, in case of a Finnish capitulation, but this was not required. Instead the unit transferred to Lithuania and deployed to stop a Russian breakthrough at Vilnius. Meanwhile reinforcements for the battalion assembled, including a Danish officer, Untersturmführer Eric Brörup from the 24th SS Motorized Regiment. In July he joined the parachute training company that was now based at Papa in Hungary and told how there was not one disciplinary case amongst the new recruits. He was issued parachute kit but because of fuel shortages 'we never got started in jump training'. There would be no further parachute jumps for the battalion and on 1 October it was officially renamed the 600th SS Parachute Battalion to remove any association with disciplinary units.

Skorzeny went from strength to strength. The Friedenthal Battalion, which was renamed 502nd SS Jäger Battalion and then Jagdverband Mitte, attracted many volunteers. Some 350 Brandenburgers joined Skorzeny's units, including Kirchner who joined Jagdverband Sued Ost. Sturmbannführer Benesch was his commander. The 600th SS Parachute Battalion was also placed under Skorzeny's command. All these units were used more as conventional infantry, however from time to time their soldiers would be selected for special missions. The SS Security Service, which had taken over the FAK in November, continued to insert agents behind enemy lines up until the very end of the war.

After Tito was established on Vis the German position in the Balkans sharply deteriorated. Operation *Rösselsprung* – the German Seventh Offensive – had been their last serious attempt to arrest the situation in the

Balkans. On 17 June Subasic, King Peter's Prime Minister in exile, visited Vis and signed an agreement that envisaged a united government with Tito. The King called on all loyal Serbs to support the partisans rather than the Chetniks. The partisans then took the war back into Serbia, hitherto an area where, partly because of the flatter terrain, success had eluded them. A free pardon to the Chetniks and Serbs that fought for the quisling Serbian General Nedic led to the collapse of the pro-German forces. In August Tito met Churchill on Capri, who again mentioned the possibility of an Allied landing in Istria, which in fact never materialized. Instead a Soviet advance through Rumania led to a staged German retreat from the Balkans and in October Belgrade was liberated. Soviet forces were within Yugoslavia's borders but Tito restricted them to one armoured corps and the deployment of advisers.

On 21 September 1944 Himmler, in a speech to military leaders, referred to Tito in the following terms: 'He has really earned his title of Marshal. When we catch him we shall kill him at once ... but I wish we had a dozen Titos in Germany, men who were leaders and had such resolution and good nerves, that, even though they were forever encircled, they would never give in. The man had nothing, nothing at all ... He was always encircled, and the man found a way out every time ... he is an uncompromising and steadfast soldier, a steadfast commander.' The story of the German attempt to capture Tito and his dramatic escape became well known throughout the Balkans both during and after the war. As Renhold wrote, 'the successful flight of the partisan leader, Tito, cemented his political position. His fame, along with other participants in the Drvar pocket, became legendary. The area became a showplace, as tourists came to view the huts and cave, which took on a museum-like character.' (The museum was destroyed in 1995 during the Bosnian war.) Surviving *Rösselsprung* contributed to Tito's reputation, which after the war enabled him to steer an independent course free from Soviet interference.

After a fierce battle for Belgrade that lasted five days partisans are seen here marching triumphantly into the capital in October 1944. Amongst their opponents had been units of the Brandenburg division. (Cody Images)

ANALYSIS

The Seventh Offensive came close to neutralizing Tito. Drvar may have been in a 'liberated area' but was vulnerable, at places only 15 miles from German ground forces, and the Germans positioned themselves in an encircling ring around it. An attack similar to Operations *Weiss* and *Schwarz* was put together, but this time Italian and Croatian units were not relied on to guard the perimeter. However, unlike previous attacks, the forces were smaller and the Germans were gambling they would be sufficient to deal with breaks into or out of the ring.

Since late 1943 the Germans, now fully realizing the importance of Tito to the partisan movement, had sought information about the location of his personal quarters in order for Special Forces to target him. The Germans selected an airborne drop. Intelligence from human intelligence sources was abundant but may not have been collated properly and the identification of the cemetery as his likely headquarters was based on the analysis of aerial photographs. Skorzeny was only brought into theatre for a few weeks and may well have been considered an outsider. If he had been told that Tito's cave was across the Unac this information was not passed on to the FAT or the Brandenburgers. Otherwise the cave would surely have been one of the initial objectives and a landing zone on top of the ridge would have been chosen. Whilst the cave, halfway up the ridge and behind a river, was well protected from an attack from the town, a landing on the top of the ridge followed by an advance down the slope would have left Tito with few options.

Even since late 1943 a smaller raid by Special Forces disguised as partisans on Tito's headquarters had been contemplated. Such an attack would have relied upon precise human intelligence for its successful resolution. Reliance on a small group of men did not sit well with the German generals and was never selected as the method of attack. However, a surveillance mission to confirm human source information and fill in intelligence gaps for the 2nd Panzer Army Ic could have been an option prior to an offensive being mounted. Deployment of Brandenburgers to have eyes on Drvar might have led to the confirmation of Tito's whereabouts prior to initiating the airborne assault. The Ic needed the trust of the commanding general if such a surveillance mission was to be mounted.

Given the imprecise nature of the intelligence available to the planners the insertion of a battalion of paratroopers to conduct the strike mission offered greater prospects for success than an ambitious hit squad. A larger force could compensate for minor intelligence or operational inadequacies. The larger the force landed in Drvar the less the Germans needed to be completely reliant on information about Tito's precise location. However, there are limits and only through sheer luck was Tito at Drvar on 25 May, rather than at his new, usual night-time residence at Bastasi, 3 miles away (a location unknown to the Germans). Because he was not under surveillance the Germans were gambling on whether Tito would be at Drvar at all.

Turning to the airborne attack, the insufficient number of transport planes and gliders initially looked like a disadvantage for Rybka; however, the availability of a company in reserve actually gave him greater flexibility. There is no evidence to suggest that Rybka envisaged a different drop zone for them and once Tito's location was identified, Rybka's decision not to redirect the second wave on to the ridge above the cave ended all hope of success for the airborne drop. As Renhold pointed out, the second wave, dropped where it was, made virtually no impact. When, during the operation, Tito's true location became apparent too much time was lost redeploying for an attack and too many paratroopers were kept behind to defend the perimeter and landing zone for the second drop.

Unlike most modern-day counterparts the airborne operation was hastily put together, in part for reasons of operational security. If the senior officers of the 500th SS Parachute Battalion were informed earlier about what was being considered more time to consider the plan would have been available. Because the unit was not part of a higher formation, like the Brandenburgers, staff support was lacking. If a Luftwaffe paratrooper formation was used then more time and effort would probably have been expended on the plan. However, because Bletchley Park found Luftwaffe signals the easiest to break, that plan might well have been fatally compromised. A higher volume of signals chatter between staffs could have compromised the operation. The Germans knew the partisans had their own agents and considered the fewer that knew of the airborne drop the better. Their cautiousness had an unexpected knock-on effect

The Fieseler Storch was a small monoplane that excelled as an observation and medical evacuation platform in mountainous terrain. Its bulbous cockpit made for a high degree of ground observation and its undercarriage absorbed the shock of short landings, enabling high vertical descents. Bombs could also be dropped. (Bundesarchiv Bild 101I11- Wisniewski - 27, Fotograf: Wisniewski)

Kumm insisted only mountain troops had any hope of defeating the partisans. Motorized formations were constrained by partisans obstructing roads and destroying bridges, and were at a disadvantage because 'the enemy simply withdraws into the mountains from roads upon which the motorized formations are advancing, in order to reappear in the rear and disrupt their rear area communications.' (Bundesarchiv Bild 101I-204-1720-04, Fotograf: Przibilla)

and helped prevent the Allies finding out about the mission, too.

Rybka was a young commander given a huge responsibility. The landing zones, so close to their chosen objectives, were laudable and bold but given the limited intelligence too much focus was given to Objective Citadel. The plan evolved on misconceptions on precisely where in Drvar Tito was located and relied too much on the fidelity of the intelligence assessments that concluded his quarters were located at the cemetery. Whether this was on Rybka's recommendation or not is unclear; perhaps the Luftwaffe commanders transporting his unit influenced where the men should land and paid more attention to the aerial photographs taken by their colleagues than Human Intelligence reports.

However, Rybka was the unit commander and given the German style of mission command we can presume his decision would have been final. He failed to compensate for limited intelligence. Given its imperfect nature a wider cordon should have been established to interdict all potential escape routes from Drvar. Perhaps the first wave was not large enough for this task and his focused approach, gambling on the fidelity of available intelligence, was the only choice he really had.

Despite successfully escaping from Drvar Tito was still vulnerable. The wider *Rösselsprung* operation could have intercepted his route to safety but for the defence put up by the partisans, in particular the 1st Proletarian Division that was facing the 7th SS Prinz Eugen Division. A 'lessons learnt' paper written by Kumm accurately identified the problems the division experienced. The warning order for the operation was only issued at 2100 on 24 May and the assembly of the 13th SS Mountain Regiment by truck through the night took time and was rushed. Regulations for the transmission of orders, as well as the provision of signals equipment, which was 'in no way sufficient for the corresponding requirements' were also criticized. Direct contact between the division and XV Mountain Corps was not established until the day of the attack. Communication between the division and its attached *panzergrenadier* battalion at Banja Luka was not achieved before the start of the operation and established only when a Fieseler Storch flew in a liaison officer. Poor knowledge of the positions of friendly units impeded economy of effort and led to friendly-fire casualties. In one instance the 7th SS Reconnaissance Battalion was stalled by heavy fire from soldiers of the 92nd Motorized Regiment. Coordination suffered, higher headquarters sometimes redirected attacks without informing their neighbours. However, some positive measures were being implemented;

divisional headquarters were in contact with the point unit through the 'assignment of a radio troop to establish direct communications from the division to the main effort battalion'.

Kumm highlighted the importance of air support in the mountains. Whilst over 400 air sorties were flown on the first day of the operation Kumm criticized the Luftwaffe for not subsequently making much of an appearance, but praised the smaller Croatian air force which 'took off at any time the division requested'. (A somewhat harsh rebuke if he knew about the damage done to airfields by Allied bombing.) The lack of sorties hampered aerial intelligence collection, which Kumm accepted 'can save the troops unnecessary marches and force dispositions' and often during partisan warfare 'must replace ground reconnaissance'. Fire support available to the troops also suffered. Kumm recognized how fighter-bomber sorties 'particularly in the mountains, can have a destructive effect on enemy march column, which often pass through mountain trails and extend for kilometres at a time'. There was a constant need for Fieseler Storch aircraft to evacuate casualties. The planes could make landings in most clearings, as occurred at Drvar, in areas where many motor vehicles could not access; however, according to Kumm they were 'only available during the beginning of the operation'. He wrote how the lack of these planes had 'a damaging effect on the morale of the *gebirgsjäger*'. Bringing in supplies by air was also recognized as an important necessity 'for the combat strength of the troops' and two Ju-52s were kept at constant readiness to provide supplies. He stressed the importance of fire discipline to conserve ammunition and ordered troops not to engage the enemy beyond 400 yards.

During *Rösselsprung* Kumm noticed increased partisan use of artillery, anti-tank guns and other heavy weapons, and recognized the effective contribution made by Allied airpower especially against 'motorized columns on the narrow, barren mountain roads'. Previously limited to the 'ineffective bombardment of cities and villages', from the second day of the operation 'the enemy was able to effectively interdict all motorized elements and supply traffic during the daytime' and 'enjoyed good success in engaging motorized columns and individual vehicles'. However this did not take the form of direct cooperation on the battlefield and there were occasions when Allied aircraft attacked partisans, mistaking them for Germans.

German commanders realized partisans survived because they prepared escape routes in advance, avoided combat on the roads and sought sanctuary in the mountains. Kumm concluded that only mountain troops stood any chance of successfully hunting them down. He thought 'an active pursuit must be taken until the enemy is exhausted and destroyed'. Once reconnaissance forces and intelligence staffs had worked out their direction of withdrawal, tactical reserves had to be brought up quickly to maintain the pursuit, for which sufficient motor transport was required. For the most part Lieutenant General Leyser stuck to this principle; however, the cordon was weak in places and vulnerable to breaking under determined counterattacks. The Germans had insufficient troop numbers to cover all escape routes and the insertion of an airborne battalion on to Tito's headquarters was an attempt to compensate for the limited reach of their ground forces.

CONCLUSION

During the partisan struggle Tito had learnt to appreciate the importance of keeping mobile. If partisans were caught in a static defence they could become surrounded; the Germans were too well supplied with ammunition for them to endure a stand-up fight. Tito took a risk at Drvar and endangered the command structure. The airborne operation was the closest any German force had come to capturing him. If successful the outcome of the partisan war probably would not have changed. However, in the medium term the Germans would have been given more freedom to operate against a confused, leaderless partisan movement. The postwar consequences would have been more striking, as the future of Yugoslavia would have been in question. Stalin may have been able to incorporate parts or all of the country into the Warsaw Pact. However, there would have been little chance of a return for the Yugoslavian monarchy, which Churchill favoured, as the communists dominated the partisan movement that effectively liberated the country.

The airborne raiding force can either be seen as too small (a proper cordon around Drvar could not be established) or too large (a force disguised as partisans infiltrating Drvar could either have attempted to seize Tito or discover his exact whereabouts for a follow on force). The judgement needs to be based on what intelligence was available to the Germans. The importance of accurate, timely intelligence in order to deploy forces effectively cannot be overstated. The planners did not know Tito's location. There was institutional rivalry within the German intelligence apparatus that set up barriers to making this happen; however, the sharing of information at working level between organizations could have mitigated the problem. The sharing of sources was not taken lightly; however, in some circumstances the benefits would outweigh the risks, particularly if operational security considerations were considered and counter-intelligence measures implemented. Operational commanders needed to be aware of intelligence gaps (for Rybka the most important of these was the location of Tito's personal quarters) and either ensure that their intelligence staffs were given all the assistance required to fill them or incorporate contingencies into the planning process to accommodate them. Intelligence

The 500th SS Battalion was untested as an airborne unit but had succeeded in surviving its baptism of fire. The unit was the obvious choice, having been created with anti-partisan operations in mind, however alternative units were available, including the Brandenburger parachute battalion. (Slovenian Museum of Contemporary History)

agencies needed to be honest about the fidelity of their sources and the veracity of their assessments if this were to happen.

The casualties suffered by the 500th SS Parachute Battalion were truly shocking. The operation was bound to be highly dangerous because, as Melson pointed out, the paratroopers had intrinsic weaknesses: stocks of supplies – ammunition, food and water – were low; once dropped their mobility was limited; heavy fire support could only be provided by air power; and in the event of failure a relieving ground force rather than withdrawal was the only hope of survival. Airborne operations needed detailed intelligence, not only about the enemy but also the terrain, and here aerial photography came into its own. With so many imponderables a ground offensive to sweep through the enemy positions was incorporated and Rendulic hoped Tito would be flushed out of hiding by the airborne attack. Rather than using the paratroopers as the hammer, he probably regarded the paratroopers more as the anvil; to be effective as the hammer required a responsiveness that only postwar airmobile troops could achieve.

BIBLIOGRAPHY

Books

Auty, Phyllis, *Tito: A Biography*, McGraw-Hill, New York (1970)

Dedijer, Vladimir, *Tito*, Simon and Schuster, New York (1950)

Foley, Charles, *Commando Extraordinary, a Biography of Otto Skorzeny*, Noontide Press, California (1988)

Franz, Rudiger W. A., *Kampfautrag: 'Bewahrüng' Das SS-Fallschirmjäger-Battalion 500/600*, Pour Le Mérite, Selent (2010)

Kahn, David, *Hitler's Spies: German Military Intelligence in World War Two*, Macmillan, New York (1978)

Kumm, Otto, *Prinz Eugen: The History of the 7th SS Mountain Division*, JJ Fedorowiz Publishing, Winnipeg (1995)

Kunzmann, A., and Milius, S., *Fallschirmjägerder Waffen-SS im Bild*, Deutsche Stimme Verlag, Riesa (2007)

Lucas, James, *Kommando: German Special Forces of World War Two*, Arms and Armour Press, London (1985)

MacLean, Fitzroy, *Disputed Barricades*, Jonathan Cape, London (1957)

MacLean, Fitzroy, *Escape to Adventure*, Little Brown and Company, Boston (1950)

Michaelis, Rolf, *SS-Fallschirmjäger-Battalion 500/600*, Schiffer Military History, Pennsylvania (2007)

Munoz, Antonio, *Forgotten Legions: Obscure Combat Formations of the Waffen-SS*, Paladin Press, Boulder (1991)

Pirjevec, Jože, *Tito in tovariši*, Cankarjeva založba, Ljubljana (2011)

Radovic, Branislav, *Operation Drvar: A Facsimile of Official Kriegsberichter Reports on the Attack by SS Fallschimjager on Tito's Headquarters May 25, 1944*, Schiffer Military History, Pennsylvania (2008)

Ritchie, Sebastian, *Our Man In Yugoslavia. The Story of a Secret Service Operative*, Frank Cass, London (2004)

Ryan, R. d'Arcy, *The Guerrilla Campaign in Yugoslavia*, Strategic and Combat Studies Institute, Camberley (1994)

Sattler, Miran, *Desant Na Drvar*, Branimar Zganjer, Zagreb (1986)

Sharp, Michael, and Westwall, Ian, *German Elite Forces*, Chartwell Books, London (2007)

Vuksic, Velimir, *Tito's Partisans*, Osprey Publishing, Oxford (2003)

Periodicals

Bennett, Ralph, 'Knight's Move at Drvar: Ultra and the attempt on Tito's Life, 25 May 1944', *Journal of Contemporary History*, vol. 22, no. 2, (April 1987): pp. 195–208

Eyre, Lieutenant Colonel Wayne D., 'Operation Rösselsprung and the Elimination of Tito, May 25, 1944: A Failure in Planning and Intelligence Support', *Journal of Slavic Military Studies*, vol. 19 (June 2006), pp. 343–76

McConville, Michael, 'Knight's Move in Bosnia and the British Rescue of Tito, 1944', *RUSI Journal* (December 1997), pp. 61–69

Melson, Charles, 'Red Sun: A German Airborne Raid, May 1944', *Journal of Slavic Military Studies*, vol. 13, no. 4 (December 2000), pp. 101–126

Wolff, Karl-Dieter, 'Das Unternehmen Rösselsprung', *Vierteljahreschete für Zeitgeschichte*, no. 4 (1970), pp. 476–509

INDEX

References to illustrations are in **bold**